Understanding
to the
Be

TOO CLOSE FOR COMFORT

Beth A. Swagman

CRC Publications
Grand Rapids, Michigan

The Scripture quotations in this publication are from the HOLY BIBLE, NEW INTERNATIONAL VERSION, copyright 1973, 1978, 1984, International Bible Society. Used by permission of Zondervan Bible Publishers.

Too Close for Comfort
Understanding and Responding to the Reality of Abuse
Copyright © 1994 by CRC Publications, 2850 Kalamazoo SE, Grand Rapids, Michigan 49560.

All rights reserved. With the exception of brief excerpts for review purposes, no part of this book may be reproduced in any manner whatsoever without written permission from the publisher. Printed in the United States of America on recycled paper. ⊕

Library of Congress Cataloging-in-Publication Data
Swagman, Beth A. 1955-
    Too close for comfort: understanding and responding to the reality of abuse / Beth A. Swagman.
        p. cm. — (Issues in Christian living)
    Includes bibliographical references.
    ISBN 1-56212-053-0 $6.25
    1. Adult child abuse victims—Religious life. 2. Adult child abuse victims—Pastoral counseling of. 3. Peer counseling in the church.
I. Title. II. Series.
BV4596.A25S935   1993
253.5—dc20   93-46973

10 9 8 7 6 5 4 3 2 1

CONTENTS

Preface 5
Introduction 7

One: It Didn't Start Overnight 9
Two: Emotional Abuse—It Hurts 21
Three: The Fifth Commandment Gone Awry 31
Four: The Unspoken Sin 39
Five: An Individual Response to Abuse 49
Six: A Community Response to Abuse 61

Appendix
    Audiovisual Resources 69
    Guidelines for All Church Members 71
    Church Policy Statements on Abuse 77

PREFACE

There are some issues in Christian living that the church *may* address—such as business ethics and family relations—and others that the church *must* address—such as divorce and remarriage and dealing with AIDS victims. The issue discussed in this booklet falls in the second category.

Numerous studies, including the one in the Christian Reformed Church that originated this booklet, have demonstrated beyond a shadow of a doubt that emotional, physical, and sexual abuse are present in our churches. Respected leaders, pastors, elders, deacons, parents, and spouses have been guilty of abusing others, and many members have been the silent victims of that abuse. This is the harsh and shameful reality. The church of Jesus Christ, the community of divine love, has been the scene of secret abuse and mistreatment.

Within the church, abuse is truly "too close for comfort." It is also too important an issue to be suppressed or ignored. Every Christian community should unite in seeking understanding, forgiveness, and healing.

The author of *Too Close for Comfort* is Beth A. Swagman, director of the Ottawa County branch of Bethany Christian Services in Western Michigan. She served as a member of the Christian Reformed Church study committee dealing with this subject.

We offer this book as a guide, within your Christian community, to self-examination and to healing.

Harvey A. Smit
Editor in chief
Education Department

INTRODUCTION

I arrived at the church about fifteen minutes before the others were scheduled to arrive. Nervously, I looked around the meeting room to make sure the chairs were arranged as I had asked. I moved the box of tissues four or five times until I was satisfied with its location. If the first woman hadn't walked in the door just at that moment, I would have raised the coffee pot for the umpteenth time to see if it was full.

This was the first morning of a support group for adult survivors of child sexual abuse. I had prayed so often for this first meeting, and I had a pretty good idea of how I wanted it to go. Instead, this was to become another lesson in letting go of my plans and letting God unfold his own agenda.

Each woman who walked into that room appeared anxious as she looked around for a comfortable spot in what would be one of the most uncomfortable moments of her life. I started the meeting by reviewing the list of expectations we would have of each other while in the support group. In my mind, I patted myself on the back for establishing a sense of safety right off the bat. I was confident now; I was in charge.

Whoosh! The roar of a rapid waterfall of grief and pain came crashing down around me. Ten of God's precious children, who had come into the room as strangers, suddenly let loose with their individual stories of being ravished by child sexual abuse. It trickled out; it spilled out; it gushed out; it filled the room. Voices quivered and eyes moistened as ten wounded hearts shared the names of their perpetrators: "my dad"; "my brother-in-law"; "the next-door neighbor"; "a minister"; "my grandpa, my dad, and all my uncles." The hour-long meeting stretched longer and longer as each survivor was given an opportunity to share the stories she had waited so many years to share.

We finally agreed to end the meeting and, after offering a few words of comfort to each other, they left me in what was once a well-manicured Sunday school classroom. Coffee cups lay everywhere. The box of tissues had been moved a few dozen times, and its remnants filled the tiny wastepaper basket. I was not confident now; I didn't want to be in charge.

Nearly fifteen months later, I am very confident that God is in charge, and since he is, I have learned that everything will be alright. This realization is not the end of a journey, but is rather the key to safe passage from one healing stage to another.

This is a book about some people's griefs, losses, and challenges. Some people grieve over relationships that started out so pleasant and so wonderful and ended in betrayal, pain, and distrust. Some people have lost significant memories of their childhood, or even the enjoyment of their childhood; other people have lost the support of family, a satisfying marital relationship, or meaningful friendships. Many people face each day challenged by the haunting thought that they are worthless, dirty, stained, and unlovable. These people have been emotionally, physically, or sexually abused or neglected. These people are also Christians.

An educator friend of mine repeats a quote he heard that goes something like this: "It takes a whole community to educate a child." I'd like to borrow that phrase to fit the purpose of this book: "It takes a whole church to help heal a survivor."

The sin of abuse is frighteningly prevalent in the Christian community. This book will help you understand the devastating impact this sin has on victims—particularly Christian victims. You will also come to understand the evil side of power that grips perpetrators—particularly Christian perpetrators. I am confident, too, that in this book you will find the key that unlocks the church's response to these hurt and wounded individuals.

—Beth A. Swagman

ONE

IT DIDN'T START OVERNIGHT

Open a newspaper any day of the week, and you're likely to read reports of abuse. The following four reports were found in one section of one daily newspaper.

- A government official was accused of abusing his power and sexually harassing his office staff. At least a dozen women came forward to protest his behavior toward them.
- A couple was convicted of starving their son to death under the pretense that starving the boy would rid him of the devil. The husband and wife had a great many supporters in the courtroom when the judge announced the verdict.
- A well-known priest accused of sexual abuse admitted that he had molested four girls nearly twenty years earlier. Although church leaders had been aware of the allegation for some time, the priest was allowed to continue in his leadership role serving other parishes. When the allegation became public, the parish he was serving at the time was reportedly divided between those who supported the priest and those who advocated for his dismissal.
- A young woman was convicted of trying to help her boyfriend break out of a minimum-security prison. The woman's lawyer told the jury that a childhood history of emotional abuse had driven the woman to such dependency that she literally fell under the control of anyone who showed the least bit of interest in her. The woman had lived with the man less than three weeks before he was caught in a robbery attempt. After his arrest and conviction, the young woman was evicted and lived

on the street, often visiting her incarcerated boyfriend. She was arrested for attempting to smuggle in various devices that the inmate hoped to use in his escape.

What Is Abuse?

The following four basic types of behavior are regarded as abusive.

Neglect

Neglect means that a caretaker has failed to provide for the safety, well-being, or basic needs of a child or dependent adult. Neglect can include failing to feed or dress someone properly, leaving someone unattended for a period of time during which harm could occur, or preventing someone from going to school or getting necessary medical care. Neglect can also involve leaving a child in the care of someone who is not capable of that responsibility, preventing someone from spending money that has been designated for his or her care or personal use, or preventing someone from taking needed medications.

Emotional

Emotional abuse occurs when someone threatens the health or emotional well-being of another. A parent threatens to leave the children home alone if they misbehave; a baby-sitter threatens to put snakes in a child's bed if the child doesn't go to sleep; a parent threatens to take away all the Christmas presents if the children don't behave quietly in church; a spouse threatens divorce if his wife becomes pregnant; a wife refuses to speak to her husband for days at a time—these are examples of emotional abuse. Name-calling, hurling insults, spreading gossip, and repeatedly swearing at someone are also considered forms of emotional abuse. This type of abuse leaves the victim feeling that he or she is no good, unwanted, worthless, or stupid.

Physical

Physical abuse occurs when a child or adult inflicts pain or injury on another person. The pain or injury inflicted is a result of the abuser's anger combined with a need to control the victim's behavior. This form of abuse often starts out as discipline, but soon goes beyond acceptable boundaries. Physical abuse takes many forms: punching, kicking, pulling hair, beating, severely spanking, or using weapons like a knife, rope, stick, or switch to inflict injury. These actions result in, but are not limited to, the victim having swollen lips, black eyes, cuts and lacerations, deep bruises, broken bones, soft tissue damage, scalds and burns, or losing consciousness.

Sexual

Sexual abuse is any act of forced intimacy upon another person. The word *forced* implies that either the adult refuses to consent to the intimacy, or—in the case of a child or teenager—cannot legally give consent to the intimacy. In Canada and in the U.S., the law states that children or teenagers under 18 cannot give consent to intimate relations because they cannot comprehend or be responsible for the sexual behavior of an adult.

The act of forced intimacy can include either physical contact, such as fondling a young boy's genitals; or nonphysical contact, such as asking the same young boy to remove his clothing for the abuser's visual stimulation. Other examples of nonphysical contact include showing pornography to children or teenagers, videotaping children engaged in sex acts, or forcing children to watch as others engage in sex acts.

Rape is sexual abuse. So is oral or anal intercourse with a child or nonconsenting adult. A spouse who refuses to engage in sexual activity with a partner can be the victim of sexual abuse if the partner persists against the spouse's wishes. Even kissing or hugging, under certain conditions, can be considered sexually abusive acts.

Who Are the Abusers?

Every human being has the potential to behave abusively. Abusers come from every race, ethnic background, nationality, social class, and economic group. Every profession, every sport, every vocational group, and every religious denomination, sect, and cult has abusers among its members. Abusers can be male or female, young or old, physically strong or physically challenged. Some abusers are but children themselves.

Despite their differences, there is one pattern that emerges in studies over and over again and that connects many of these perpetrators. The majority of abusers, at least once before in their lives, were themselves victims of abuse.

The Discomfort Zone

When we read stories of abuse in our newspapers, we tend to have one of three reactions:

• We don't want to believe the stories we've read.

• We tend to shift some blame to the victim for contributing to the abuse in some way. We surmise that perhaps the young woman was in a questionable place or out late at night unaccompanied. It seems so unbelievable that a person would commit rape without having been encouraged in some way.

• We find ourselves sympathetic to the abuser, whose name is now splashed all over the newspaper. "What if the allegations are false?" we ask ourselves. "That person's reputation could be ruined."

We probably react in these ways to avoid the discomfort zone. Acknowledging one person's inhumane treatment of another person is extremely difficult. Even more uncomfortable is to imagine oneself in the place of the victim who was subjected to such humiliation and injury. Could anything be more uncomfortable than knowing the victim and seeing her at the grocery store or in the library? What does one say to such a person?

Perhaps nothing moves us more into the discomfort zone than recognizing that the same unspeakable abuses we have read about in the newspapers are being committed by Christians against other Christians—people who sit with us right in our own churches. How can these crimes happen in Christian homes? Aren't people who attend church and believe in God immune from these sins?

Facts Don't Lie

We usually tend to think that these tragic events only affect the lives of people living "someplace else." In all honesty, our inclination is to brush off these stories a little too quickly while telling ourselves that such things could never happen where *we* live. We don't want to think that our children go to school with other children who are victims of abusive teachers, neighbors, police officers, parents, or relatives. Likewise, we don't like the unsettling feeling that employers in *our* community would physically, emotionally, or sexually violate their employees.

Nevertheless, there it is in the newspaper! A parish priest confesses to fondling several altar boys. Several former members of a congregation accuse the pastor of abusing them during privately scheduled catechism classes. A young Christian mother is convicted of locking her six-year-old in the closet and denying him food and drink for several hours because he continued to wet the bed at night.

The Christian community has a hard time recognizing that real stories of abuse can be found within its boundaries. We're reluctant to admit that some parents just don't have the knack of parenting, and that they can leave some dreadful scars on their children. But we tend to blame outside factors for abusive behavior within the Christian community—such things as alcoholism, pornography, over-strict upbringing, or a dysfunctional home life. Whatever our justification for its presence, one fact remains—abuse does exist within the church.

In recent times, the Roman Catholic Church has found itself dealing with scores of incidents in which parishioners have accused priests of misusing their authority and abusing their constituents. Reports indicate that the Roman Catholic Church has paid out several million dollars in claims brought by parishioners against their parish priests.

Protestant churches are also facing the painful task of uncovering abuse within their church families and within their church walls. In Canada, the Anglican Church has reacted to similar alleged offenses by instituting several new policies setting appropriate limits for interaction between church leaders and their congregations. These new church policies also lay out specific courses of action that a church member can take if he or she believes that inappropriate behavior has taken place.

The Mennonite Church has responded to allegations made by its members by developing detailed and informative materials to educate pastors, church leaders, lay leaders, and church members on the nature of abuse. These materials include liturgies, articles, suggestions to pastors, statistics sheets, and reading lists, and are available at low cost to anyone who requests them.

The Christian Reformed Church, a 350,000-member denomination with churches throughout the United States and Canada, is another example of a Protestant denomination that is responding to the crisis of abuse. In 1989, members of this denomination's governing body, or *synod*, heard stories of abuse that was taking place in the homes of Christian Reformed church members. One of the tragic stories involved the violation of the pastor/member relationship. This synod responded by appointing a committee to study the problem of abuse within the denomination.

As committee members began exploring the subject, they quickly agreed that the problem of abuse did exist within the denomination; the next task was trying to determine to what extent the abuse had occurred. For that information the committee went to the denomination's college—Calvin College—to request that its Social Research Center conduct a survey of 1000 church members. Of those surveys, 643 were returned, and the committee soon had the stunning results.

The survey showed that 12 percent of the denomination's adult members had identified themselves as victims of physical abuse, 13 percent as victims of sexual abuse, and 19 percent as victims of emotional abuse. Many of the respondents reported suffering more than one form of abuse. The Social Research Center determined that 28 percent of the adult population of the church (nearly 64,000 men and women!) had identified themselves as victims of abuse.

The survey also addressed the issue of who did the abusing. Fifteen percent of the adult population of the denomination identified themselves as abusers. These were trusted parents, family members, church leaders, neighbors, and other authority figures. Many of the adult perpetrators also disclosed that they had been victims of abuse in their childhood or adolescence.

As hard as it may be for us to accept, the results of the survey clearly show that abuse happens to people just like you and me, both Christian and non-Christian. Perhaps even more difficult to accept is that the abusers are also people just like you and me. As more and more Christians wake up to these harsh realities, more and more churches and denominations will be moved to acknowledge the existence of abuse in their church families and within their church walls. The fact that many church organizations are looking into this matter is a significant step toward dealing with this horrible reality.

Denial

It's crucial that the church, Christ's agent of healing on earth, face up to the reality of abuse. When we fail to acknowledge abuse in the Christian community, the victims of that abuse cannot receive the support they so desperately need. We Christians who are uncomfortable with the subject tend to subtly tell the victim to forget what has happened, or to forgive the abuser so that both parties can get on with life. In doing so, we revictimize the victim. The victim often feels ashamed and blames him- or herself, making it more difficult to begin a healing journey. More often than not, this victim will choose to leave the congregation rather than suffer the humiliation of disbelief or deal with the frustration of being told to forget the past.

But denial also creates another, very dangerous, situation. When we deny the existence of abuse, we're prevented from confronting the abuser. And as long as the denial continues, the abuser has tacit permission to continue the abuse—that means that more children, adolescents, and adults are placed at risk. The threat of more abuse is horrible enough; but realize also that without confrontation, the abuser's healing journey cannot begin either. The role of the church is not to impede healing, but rather to facilitate it. Healing is a main component of the message of salvation that evangelical Christians so strongly grasp.

Sometimes we deny abuse in order to avoid the blame for what is happening. Consider the family of a 42-year-old man who held his victim captive in an underground vault. The man's family apparently denied that the man had problems and subsequently failed to enter his living quarters for months. While in the end it was the 42-year-old man who was arrested and held on abuse charges, the family needs to shoulder some of the blame for having denied that a problem even existed.

The Christian community needs to distinguish the difference between accepting full responsibility for something they have not done and taking up the responsibility to tell both victims and abusers that healing and forgiveness are available through Jesus Christ. In short, the Christian community needs to face up to the reality of abuse and then do something about it.

The Hazards of the Pedestal

There were nearly thirty children in my kindergarten class. As we grew up together, we passed candy around to each other on birthdays, took turns at safety patrol, stood awkwardly around our lockers hoping that our latest crush wouldn't see a pronounced pimple, and signed yearbooks promising to remain best friends forever.

Most of us went on to college and careers. Now, after all those years of addressing each other by our first names and nicknames, we find ourselves in adulthood with titles coming between us. Keith is now called Reverend, and Joan is now called Doctor. Titles tend to put people on pedestals that somehow separate them from people who do not have titles other than Mr., Mrs., Ms., or Miss.

Of course, acknowledging the gifts and accomplishments of adults who have worked hard to get where they are is fitting. It is even appropriate to personally address them with a title they have sought after and earned. But sometimes we treat such people as if their titles magically give them privileges that others do not enjoy.

This tendency to put people on pedestals can be dangerous for the Christian community. We tend to close our eyes to titled people who abuse their authority or commit sins of abuse. Sometimes it seems that titled persons enjoy protection from accusation that others do not have. For the victim, bringing an abuse allegation against such a person becomes much more risky; there can be immense social pressure to keep the titled person intact on his or her pedestal. As a result, fewer victims come forward when the alleged abuser has a title or position of authority—particularly in the church. Victims of alleged abuse by a church leader are often submitted to serious cross-examination and are sometimes even accused of causing dissention among church members.

"Pedestal people" tend to surround themselves with others who are dedicated to keeping the base of the pedestal firm at all costs. These faithful people are often willing to come to the defense of the pedestal person, even if they have no knowledge of that person's activities. For some Christians, the pedestal *alone* is worth defending. In such cases the victim has an extremely difficult time being heard and believed. And the alleged abuser, insulated from confrontation, often goes on to abuse another.

Once a person has been elevated to a pedestal, he or she is particularly susceptible to becoming either an emotional, physical, or sexual abuser. Church leaders can even commit *spiritual* abuse, using their power and authority in the church to manipulate people and situations. Tragically, when spiritual abuse takes place, many of the victims choose to leave the church. They often become alienated from God, convinced that if abuse could come from a church leader, then God certainly must not care what happens to his people.

Headship

The principle of headship can produce a similar power hierarchy.

In some churches, men and women play distinctively different roles. Men are given the final authority to make decisions that affect the church family and government. The men of the church are responsible for providing spiritual leadership, dispensing funds to meet financial needs, and, when necessary, overseeing the discipline of the family at home or at church. In such churches, women are expected to adhere to the authority of men, and they encourage their children to comply with the authority of men as well. The woman takes a submissive role, acknowledging her husband as the head of the family and men as the leaders in the church.

Such a strong headship principle, while setting forth distinctive roles, sometimes becomes a justification for abusive behavior because it assumes that one gender must submit to the authority of the other. This principle, taken out of its biblical context, has permitted women to be beaten for questioning how the family income is spent or for asserting their desire to make purchases independently of their spouse. Some male abusers justify absolutely irrational demands by pointing to the headship principle in Scripture. Following are two such examples:

A middle-aged father had sexual intercourse with each of his three daughters when they became teenagers. He claimed it was his role as a father to teach his daughters how to please a husband. He further justified his actions by stating that it was better for his daughters to learn this lesson from their father than from a boyfriend. He knew the Bible would forbid premarital intercourse with a boyfriend, but he could not be convinced that his own behavior with his daughters was unbiblical and sinful.

A husband severely beat his wife when the Thanksgiving turkey was not ready on time; the delay interfered with his plan to watch a football game on television. The wife reheated the turkey after the game ended, but the husband complained the turkey was too dry and hurled it across the room at his spouse. He narrowly missed her, but struck a four-year-old child who had come into the kitchen to get a snack. The child was taken to a local medical facility and received several stitches to close a gash on his forehead. The physician treating the child was told that the child had disobeyed his father's warning not to run in the house.

Often the headship principle prevents victims of abuse from coming forward with their stories. These victims feel that they cannot claim abuse by a father or male relative because doing so would dishonor their parents and those in authority over them. Such victims end up with a distorted view of male authority, which causes tremendous conflict in their spiritual life. How can they think of God as their loving Father when that image brings about nothing but pain and confusion?

Human Sexuality vs. Sex

For many people, few things are as difficult to talk about as sex. But it wasn't always that way. We read in Genesis 2 that Adam and Eve were both naked and neither of them felt ashamed. As with everything else in that garden paradise, they recognized God as the founder and creator of their sexuality. They felt no embarrassment about having sexual organs or about expressing their sexuality toward each other. After the fall of this first family, God gave us marriage as an institution within which we could safely and fully explore the very special gift of our sexuality.

But with the fall, everything changed. The pages of Scripture are filled with examples of the way the purpose of human sexuality was distorted. And today—more than ever, it seems—that gift is openly corrupted.

Today we tend to refer to human sexuality by its cruder term: *sex*. Sex can refer to an act of intimacy or an impulsive act of self-gratification. Our society does not refer to sex as a gift, but rather as a skill to acquire as soon as one is able. Obviously, that idea goes against God's intentions. The term *sexuality* connotes maturity, honesty, comfort, responsibility, and mutual respect. The term *sex* connotes something cheap, quick, dirty, and secretive.

Historically, the church has shied away from defining sexuality as a gift to be treasured and safely explored in the context of a monogamous relationship. Instead, the church has often held the opinion (at least in practice) that sexuality is to be suppressed or denied or kept within the secret confines of the bedroom. In short, sex is not an appropriate topic for public discussion for most Christians. That being the case, many churches have failed to offer guidance to couples on how to explore the gift of sexuality within marriage. The church is also usually silent when the time comes to share that knowledge with young children and adolescents.

Since the church in general has a difficult time dealing with sex, the hardest form of abuse for the church to acknowledge and handle is sexual abuse. Why? Because it forces Christians to delve into the most private lives of church and family members. It forces Christians to look at the darker side of humanity. Confronting an abuser with such allegations is extremely difficult, especially when the abuser is well thought of or holds a position of power. And helping the victim cope with his or her feelings of being contaminated and dirty can also be a perplexing problem. As we've said before, dealing with sexual abuse forces those who have to face both the perpetrators and the victims out of their comfort zones.

Last Thoughts

The Christian community has a hard time accepting its vulnerability to the sin of abuse. As long as we refuse to recognize its existence, we can justify doing nothing for the victims who suffer from our ignorance and apathy. As long as we refuse to recognize that there are abusers among us, we can pretend to escape responsibility for their continuing attacks on children and adults.

Christ is still the head of the church. He knows when the members of his body are hurting and he calls the Christian community to make a difference in the lives of these people. As we learn how to respond to both the abused and the abuser, we can fulfill our responsibilities as healers and comforters. Let us make a difference where we can.

Suggestions for Group Session

Getting Started

Begin by joining together in prayer. Pray that God will allow everyone present to be open and honest during this study of abuse. Pray also that God will gradually reveal any area of our lives that needs to change, either because we were abused or because we abused others in some way.

After prayer, introduce yourselves and lay some ground rules for your sessions together. Assure the group that whatever is revealed through this study will be held in strictest confidence. Also, make your group a forum for accepting and dealing with the emotions that surround abusive situations. Assure those who have gathered that it's alright to be discouraged, ashamed, sad, angry—no matter what, they can feel safe expressing those emotions within this group. Reiterate the fact that the church is a place of healing, and tell the members that you earnestly desire that healing begin here in this group.

Before you begin, you might want to ask group members to share what brought them to this particular study. Each member of this study group has a reason for desiring to learn more about abuse. Each reason is personal, so if someone chooses not to share his or her reason, respect that decision.

Group Discussion and Activity

We've listed several activities and questions—too many for most groups to use in one session. Please be selective! As a group, you know best which questions and activities will fit your time frame and interests.

From Chapter One

1. Have group members take turns reading from the list of examples of abuse found in the beginning of this chapter. Be sure to include all four types of abuse.

2. Take a few minutes for group members to express how they felt when the list was being read.

3. The list of abuses you have read is not nearly a complete list. Take some time as a group to share other examples of abuses they've read or heard about.

4. Many survivors of abuse have been compared to survivors of the Holocaust, survivors of a tragic accident or natural disaster, or survivors of war. What do survivors of abuse have in common with survivors of these other disasters?

From the Newspaper

Distribute sections of a daily newspaper (either local or regional) and have each person look for stories of abuse. Allow time for reading, then report on the stories. On newsprint, a blackboard, or an overhead projector, take note of who the alleged perpetrators were. After everyone has shared a news story, discuss any common characteristics you noted as the alleged perpetrators were identified and described. Try to come up with a profile of an abuser.

From Your Experience

This chapter describes the efforts several denominations have made to develop a coordinated response to abuse.

1. A couple of individuals should summarize for the group how some specific denominations are responding to abuse.

2. How is your congregation responding to abuse? What else, if anything, needs to be done?

From the Bible

Read Genesis 4:2b-8; Genesis 37:3-5, 19-20, 26-32; 2 Samuel 11:1-4, 14-17. As a group, answer the following questions. You may have questions or doubts you would also like to raise and discuss as they relate to the passages. If you have a particularly large group, you could divide the passages between a few smaller groups.

1. In these passages, why do you think people abused others?

2. Could these abusers have gotten what they wanted without acting abusively?

3. Were the abusers caught? Were they penalized?

4. Rarely does abuse take place without someone's knowledge, or at least suspicion, that something odd is going on. In any of these stories, did someone else know about the abuse? Was there an accomplice in any of these stories? If so, how does the accomplice react to the abuse?

5. Describe Reuben's role in the story of Joseph (Genesis 37:3-5, 19-20.)

6. Describe Israel's response when he saw Joseph's coat. Do you think he was being abused by his sons in their deliberate attempt to fool him?

Read James 1:13-16.

1. According to James, who is responsible for a sinner's actions?

2. What happens when sin is allowed to continue?

3. What are we doing to ourselves when we fail to accept responsibility for our own sins?

Closing Prayer

Abuse is a very painful topic within the Christian community. In sentence prayers, group members may ask the Lord to bless his church, to heal it and the survivors within it, to heal any abusers within it, and to be compassionate toward all those who are in some way affected by abuse.

Please read chapter two for next time. Come prepared to discuss your reading in your group.

TWO

EMOTIONAL ABUSE—IT HURTS

When 16-year-old Anna first walked in the door, her therapist was struck by the blank look in her beautiful blue eyes. At first glance, her therapist could tell that Anna came from a wealthy family. She wore a leather skirt and a designer-label sweater, and looked like a girl who would be the envy of her peers. Yet something was different about Anna: she stared at the floor throughout the session, intentionally avoiding eye contact with the therapist. And she complained about her family and friends from the moment she sat down until the moment she walked out the door.

She said that she had a poor relationship with her parents and that she hated her brother. As she perceived it, he was spoiled rotten and, as far as her parents were concerned, could do no wrong. Anna talked angrily about both her mother and father. She claimed that neither one loved her.

But how could that be? Outwardly, one would have thought that her parents doted on her. Every session she wore something new, and she drove to therapy sessions in a sporty red subcompact. At sixteen, she had more material possessions than many adults. But it was clear that, despite her possessions, Anna was a very unhappy young woman. In the sessions that followed Anna alternated between hostility, dejection, and frustration.

After several sessions of listening to Anna speak angrily about nearly everyone she knew, the therapist decided it was time to gently move Anna past the complaints to the issues. What they uncovered together was a lifetime of emotional abuse.

The therapist found out that Anna was adopted shortly after birth by a successful businessman and his wife. They had a biological son who was then three years old, and had chosen to adopt their next child after the wife had experienced life-threatening complications during her son's birth.

Anna's earliest memories were of conflicts between herself and her brother. But what should have been a normal sibling relationship was thrown off balance by Anna's father and mother. Whenever Anna fought with her brother, she was forced to choose a toy from her room to throw in the wastebasket. When Anna would refuse, her father would zoom in on a favorite toy, heave it into the basket, and storm out of the room. Anna's mother would then enter and take her aside. She would console her daughter with an offer to go shopping if only Anna would stop crying and be good. During those shopping trips, the favorite toy that had been lost would be replaced with something else. But Dad was not to know. The new toy had to be hidden from Dad or it too would end up in the trash.

Anna spent more and more time alone in her room playing with toys that she feared her father would throw away. The pattern of having to sacrifice a toy after fighting with her brother continued until Anna entered junior high school.

Anna also told the therapist about how her father called her names and taunted her. He frequently reminded Anna that she was adopted from an immoral woman. Her father began calling her "little slut" at an early age. In contrast, he consistently referred to Anna's brother as "my own son."

According to Anna, another of her father's favorite names for her was (what I will euphemistically translate as) his "little piece of cow manure." Anna's mother confirmed that her husband used the name frequently. One particularly bitter memory for Anna occurred on the evening of her first high school prom. As her date stood in the doorway, her father mockingly referred to her using this pet name. Anna was mortified and ran upstairs in tears. Anna's mother followed her upstairs to her room where she promised Anna yet another shopping trip if she would dry up her tears, accept her dad's teasing, and have a good time. Anna remembers this occasion as the last time she complied with her mother's pleading for peace in the family.

That summer, Anna began to hang around some kids from school who were known to be involved with drugs and alcohol. She experimented with these substances on several occasions and repeatedly broke curfew. Each night when she came home she was subjected to a barrage of degrading accusations and insults from her father. He loudly reminded her on several occasions that her biological mother was, in his opinion, a whore; after which he accused her of following in her mother's footsteps. Each confrontation ended with Anna's father, red in the face from yelling, hurling insults at Anna as she walked up the stairs.

Anna traded in her designer wardrobe for black jeans, black tee shirts, black sweaters, and black jewelry. Her blonde hair contrasted sharply with *the heavy black eye makeup that she chose to wear. Relatives and friends blamed the changes in Anna on her new friends.*

Meanwhile Anna's father continued the threats and name-calling. But his attempts to control her behavior with punishments were totally ineffective. If Anna was grounded, she simply refused to come home from school on Friday, and was not heard from again until Monday morning when she would show up in school. Her parents filed several police reports listing Anna as a runaway. After several visits with a probation officer, Anna and her family were referred to counseling.

What Is Emotional Abuse?

Anna's story is just one example of emotional abuse—one person using threats and fear to control another person's life. Emotional abuse involves destroying a person's feeling of self-worth through harassment or through depriving that person of something. The victim lives with the constant threat of physical violence or loss, and his or her safety, well-being, and ability to trust is severely undermined. The abuser weakens the victim's mental ability to resist, to defend himself or herself, or to ask the help of others to protest the abuse. In the end, emotional abuse reinforces a sense of helplessness in the victim and makes him or her dependent on the abuser. (Taken from the Report to Synod from the Committee to Study Abuse in the Christian Reformed Church; see appendix).

Anna's story is not unique or uncommon. According to the survey conducted for the Christian Reformed Church, emotional abuse was the highest reported form of abuse within that denomination. Nineteen percent of the adult membership of the denomination confessed to being victims of emotional abuse.

Emotional Abuse Doesn't Stand Alone

Emotional abuse does not usually occur on its own; it accompanies other kinds of abuse with sickening regularity. Many sexual abusers threaten their victims with violence if they tell. And many physical abusers verbally insult and ridicule their victims, call them names, and threaten them.

Emotional abuse accompanies sexual or physical abuse because it serves to

- convince the victim that the abuser isn't all bad.
- manipulate the victim into not reporting the incident.
- manipulate the victim into not resisting or fighting back.
- encourage feelings of helplessness which may lead to future incidents of abuse.
- confirm the disdain the abuser has for the victim.
- confirm for the abuser that the victim somehow deserves what is about to take place.

But not all emotional abuse involves negative threats and degradation. Emotional abuse also takes place when children are rewarded with a prize or toy for allowing other abusive activities to continue. Anna was "rewarded" with shopping sprees for keeping peace in the family. Adult abusers bribe children into sexual activity. Teenagers are rewarded with clothes, drugs, alcohol, or participation in school activities if only they will submit to sexual acts or star in a pornographic video. Remorseful spouse abusers often comfort their victims with something like a new coat or new carpet. Sometimes abusers will even nurse the bruises they have inflicted.

"You're Taking It Too Seriously"
People are sometimes critical of victims of emotional abuse. They feel that they're too defensive or too touchy, and that they should just lighten up a bit. Unfortunately, a person who thinks a victim is too defensive can sometimes be *too* convincing, forcing the victim to minimize the pain he or she feels: "He was just kidding. What's the matter—can't you take a little joke?"

Sometimes the victims themselves minimize the effect of abuse. There appears to be less of a stigma attached to being an emotionally abused person than there is to being a physically or sexually abused person. Emotional abuse victims tend to be more cavalier about it. An adult who was victimized by a parent may say, "Dad said that kind of stuff to everybody. No one really took him seriously. That was just Dad's way." Or, "Mom said those things when she got really mad, and usually I or one of my sisters made her angry. We just let it go in one ear and out the other." Victims are also more willing to discuss emotional abuse because they're not afraid that the abuser will suffer any consequences.

When the abuser or the community labels a victim of emotional abuse as being too sensitive, not having a sense of humor, or not being able to let things go, then the abuser and the community promote the lie that emotional abuse does not hurt anyone, or that its effects are short-lived.

We Can't Take It Seriously Enough
We may have a hard time accepting the stories of victims who have been physically and sexually abused. Unfortunately, many of us have a harder time accepting emotional abuse as abusive. Because emotional abuse is seen as a "lesser evil" than physical or sexual abuse, victims are afraid of not being believed and are therefore more hesitant to como forward to tell their story and to begin a healing journey.

But there's another sad twist to this form of abuse. Since emotional abuse is usually the most visible symptom of other forms of abuse, and since people tend to minimize its effect, victims can also have a very difficult time reporting other forms of abuse. If the community won't believe that the alleged abuser is guilty of emotional abuse, why would the community believe he or she is guilty of another type of abuse?

Consider Anna's story again as a case in point. Although Anna didn't like the names and insults her father used, she never described his activity as abusive, and neither did her mother. What she did label as abusive were her dad's *physical* attacks. In later therapy sessions Anna shared that her father had often kicked her, leaving bruises on her buttocks and on the backs of her legs. The attacks worsened in intensity once Anna had made up her mind not to obey her father and mother. Both mother and daughter claim that some of the worst attacks came after the police had returned Anna home after a weekend out with friends.

Anna acknowledged that she would never have reported her father for physical abuse. Because of his position in the community, she didn't believe that anyone would believe her or come to her aid. How much less would they believe her claims about emotional abuse?

Reports of emotional abuse must be taken seriously. They represent serious violations of trust and personal dignity. What's more, they may indicate that the victim is undergoing other forms of abuse that are more difficult to acknowledge. Taking emotional abuse seriously will encourage victims to come out of hiding and to begin a healing journey. Acknowledging the seriousness of emotional abuse may also empower a victim to react to his or her situation and prevent it from moving to another, more physically harmful stage.

Sticks and Stones Can Break My Bones . . .

Words and threats cannot injure the human body the way sticks and stones can. There is no apparent damage to ears that hear threats or insults. A child's eyes are not damaged when he watches a parent destroy his pet. A woman's arm is not bruised or twisted when a boyfriend threatens suicide to keep the relationship alive. The damage inflicted by emotional abuse is not external, but internal. And broken hearts don't mend as easily as bruised muscles.

Connie is a 42-year-old woman and a survivor of emotional abuse. In her case the abuse was perpetrated by her father and two older brothers from the time she was very young until she left home at age 17.

Since she couldn't afford college after high school, she worked in a diner outside of town and found an apartment with two other waitresses. Connie was attracted to the truckers who came to the diner. They paid attention to her and bolstered her self-image. To one who had endured years of degradation and humiliation, their advances were a welcome change. Connie felt particularly flattered by one trucker's compliments. One day, that trucker lured Connie into his rig and assaulted her. After the incident, the trucker never returned to the diner. Nine months later, Connie delivered her first child—a daughter.

Connie still works at the diner, but her depressed appearance results in few tips. And although she is a grown woman, she still feels deeply the results of that early abuse.

You Just Can't Please Some People

You will remember the feelings Anna had toward both her parents. The fear and anger that she felt were the result of years of insults and inappropriate personal accusations. No matter what Anna did, she could never convince her father that she wasn't like her birth mother. Even when she behaved appropriately, she couldn't change his opinion. And when she decided to stop trying to please him, he got even angrier. Anna felt trapped and helpless, and her mother contributed to her feelings of inadequacy. She led her daughter to believe that she wasn't good enough because she couldn't stop her father's outbursts. Anna couldn't trust her parents to behave rationally.

Emotional abuse destroys the relationship between the abuser and the abused. Love and affection are replaced with hatred and fear. The child who feels guilty for making the parent so angry vows to behave better or differently. Imagine the confusion that he or she feels when the improved behavior still does not end the parent's rage. Children who grow up constantly trying to out-guess an abusive person soon become depressed, anxious, and hesitant to reach out to others. Victims of emotional abuse consistently report that forming relationships with others is difficult because of strong feelings of suspicion and distrust.

A child such as Anna, who is emotionally abused, can't look to parents or caregivers for help in developing self-esteem and self-respect. As the child tries harder and harder to earn positive reinforcement, he or she soon tries to fill the needs of the abuser at the expense of his or her own needs. But no matter how hard the child tries, the abuser doesn't respond positively. In this case, intimacy is hampered by fear of betrayal and suspicion that the other person won't remain honest.

Just as childhood relationships are damaged by emotional abuse, so are adult relationships. The marital relationship is devastated when one partner chooses to manipulate, harass, threaten, or control the other partner. Intimacy levels decrease substantially as the victim withdraws in order to find the strength to live through the next barrage of insults and threats. Fear and suspicion actually run the marriage, and both partners can begin to feel trapped and hopeless. As life drags on, the victim may treasure time away from the abuser and may also turn to compulsive and addictive behaviors to numb the pain of being treated so cruelly. And some people go to even further extremes.

Jerry was 51 years old when he came for counseling. Over the course of the therapy he told a story of emotional abuse that began in his youth and continued into his marriage. When he was young, Jerry's parents re-

quired that he take care of his younger siblings—no small task, since Jerry was the oldest of seven children. Jerry was not allowed to play outside with other neighborhood boys if one of his siblings needed him in the house. He was also kept from extracurricular activities such as sports and band. When he tried out for and made the middle school basketball team, his mother told him there was no way he would be allowed to spend so many afternoons away from home. Jerry told the coach his ankle was hurting him and then quit the team.

Jerry left home at the age of 17 and entered the Marines. No longer welcome at home, Jerry searched for comfort and security. He married a woman he had met on leave, and within a few short years they had three children. But his marriage was hindered by the same demanding atmosphere that he had experienced at his parent's home. Throughout the marriage, Jerry said he worked day and night to please Carla, but it was never enough. Carla spent more money than Jerry made; as a result, Jerry worked more. When he worked more, Carla complained that he was away from home too much.

After seventeen years of marriage, Carla asked for a divorce. Again without a place to live, Jerry moved a cot into the back of the shop he ran. Jerry became very lonely and attempted suicide by carbon monoxide poisoning. One of Jerry's customers found Jerry in his car in the garage and called the police. The police recommended counseling, and now Jerry is trying to put the pieces of his life back together.

The Shame of Emotional Abuse

Emotional abuse is devastating to the victim because he or she is so often humiliated—both in private and in public. Parents threaten children in grocery stores; teachers criticize students mercilessly in front of other students; coaches ridicule their players in front of spectators; spouses fight and say cruel things to each other in front of their children. Remember how Anna was humiliated by her father in front of her boyfriend?

When a person is continually degraded and humiliated, the names and descriptions can start to stick. The victim can come to adopt these descriptions and behave accordingly. And that's when emotional abuse does its most devastating damage.

Lack of Evidence

Emotional abuse is also devastating to its victims because no tangible evidence exists that the threats or words or manipulations occurred. Even child-protection agencies that investigate allegations of abuse against children report that it is extremely difficult, if not impossible, to substantiate allegations of emotional abuse.

It's terribly frustrating for victims of emotional abuse to feel in their hearts the horrible damage that others have inflicted, knowing that no one will believe them if they report it. Such circumstances can lead the emotionally abused victim to deny that the abuse had an impact on them—or that it even occurred. Victims who deny abuse cannot find healing for themselves or forgiveness for the abuser.

As a caring Christian community, we must respond to allegations of emotional abuse. First we need to affirm the victim's story and take it seriously. Then we must carefully examine the allegations. We must recognize that the devastation behind emotional abuse lies not in the physical realm, but in the heart. The abuse may well be away from our sight and hearing, but it must definitely be within our believing.

Suggestions for Group Session

Getting Started

Begin this session by taking turns reading the verses of 1 John 4:7-12. Then join together in prayer, praying that God will make the information in this session clear in the minds of group members. Pray that God will help you to show Christian love and sensitivity to each other as you deal with the topic of emotional abuse. Ask the Lord to open your hearts, giving you insight into what constitutes emotional abuse and courage to deal with it.

After the opening prayer, read together the following words from "Our World Belongs to God," the Contemporary Testimony of the Christian Reformed Church:

[We are] the Bride of Christ,
his chosen partner,
loved by Jesus and loving him:
delighting in his presence,
seeking him in prayer,
silent before the mystery of his love.

Group Discussion and Activity

Please take a moment to jot down what you think emotional abuse actually is, and give one or two examples that support your ideas. Then share your writing with other group members. No one should criticize or contradict what another group member has said; at this point in the session the group should be open, and should receive all ideas as valid.

From Chapter Two

1. Discuss the effects of emotional abuse on Anna.

2. Do you think Anna was justified in her rebellious actions? Why or why not?

28

3. Share with the group what you might have done if Anna had come to you for help.

4. How did the nature of Anna's relationship with her parents affect the rest of her life? (Think about how critical she was of her friends as well as of her family.)

While many people associate emotional abuse with cruel words, some persons are abused when a loved one chooses to give them the "silent treatment."

1. Why do people choose to be silent for extended periods of time?

2. What effect does silence have on the victim? On others in the house or at the office?

From Your Experience

A well-known comedian has made quite a reputation reciting his one-line complaint: "I don't get no respect . . . no respect at all!" For victims of emotional abuse, this line cuts like a knife. These people have often pleaded with the church to affirm the pain they have suffered. But alas, they get no respect because there is no outward evidence that they've been hurt. While the pain may not be physical, the abuse is no less hurtful or damaging. Emotional abuse is a formidable foe. Respect its victims!

Most of the people in your group will attest to being a victim of emotional abuse at least once in their lives. With the group, try to complete the following activity openly and honestly.

1. If you are able, share with the group an incident of emotional abuse committed against you.

2. Share with the group how you felt at the time the abuse occurred.

3. Have you shared this before with anyone?

4. Be sure to affirm each other in the group. It takes courage to share a story of abuse.

From the Bible

The book of James is a good resource for studying how God wants us to relate to one another. Read James 1:26-27; 2:12-17; 3:1-6, 17-18; 4:1-3, 11-12.

1. What kinds of behavior displease God?

2. How does God expect us to communicate with one another?

3. After reading these verses in James, which of your own behaviors would you like to change? Please write them down on a piece of paper.

4. If you wish, share what you have written down and then encourage each other to follow through.

Closing Prayer

   Pray for healing for those members of the group who have identified that they have been hurt by emotional abuse. Pray too that all of us will learn how to communicate better with others, showing love to one another in all situations.

THREE

THE FIFTH COMMANDMENT GONE AWRY

When It All Falls Apart

Bob and Michelle met and dated in high school. They eloped six months after graduation, when Bob received his orders to report for active duty in Vietnam. Michelle conceived a child during the brief time she and Bob were together before Bob left. When Bob returned from his tour of duty, his daughter Sandy was two years old.

Bob and Michelle had a difficult time readjusting to one another when Bob returned. Michelle had worked while Bob was gone and had made a successful life for herself and her baby. Naturally, little Sandy was more comfortable with her mother than with her father, who was almost a stranger to her. Sandy preferred her mother to feed her, change her clothes, and play with her. Bob resented the fact that his own daughter felt uncomfortable with him and called her spoiled when she refused to sit on his lap or play with him.

Bob and Michelle had another daughter, Kelly, fifteen months after Bob's return to the United States. Seeing an opportunity to start fresh with this child, Bob favored Kelly. He held her and fed her and changed her, always reassuring her of his love and devotion.

The couple grew further apart after Kelly's birth. As Sandy grew older, Bob began to doubt that Sandy was his child. Bob grew more suspicious of his wife, and began to accuse Michelle of having an affair while he was gone. Soon he had convinced himself that his accusations were true, and he refused to sleep with her because she was unfaithful. To get away from the tension, Michelle took her old job back. She enjoyed the time away from her home.

But Bob's suspicions grew. Having convinced himself that Michelle was having another affair, he tried to catch her in the act. He became obsessed with knowing where his wife was at all times, and he accused her repeatedly of being unfaithful.

He called Michelle at work precisely one minute after the eight minutes he had allotted for her to drive to work, park the car, and get to her office. If she was not available, Bob called every minute after that until she arrived. When they finally connected, Bob raged at Michelle for not getting to work on time. Sometimes he called her a whore, accusing her of being with another man. Bob threatened to report her to her boss for having affairs with company employees.

One day when Michelle was a few minutes late arriving home from work, Bob's jealousy turned physically abusive. He struck Michelle about the face and pulled her hair until she was on her knees in pain. She pleaded with Bob to let her go, but he shouted that his actions were justified—he needed to punish his disobedient wife. At Bob's insistence, Michelle promised that she would never speak to another man, if only he would stop hurting her. During the next few days, Bob was contrite and apologetic to Michelle. But he still maintained that Michelle needed to be taught a lesson—he would not have hurt her if she had not disobeyed him.

But Michelle was not the only victim of Bob's physically abusive behavior; Sandy often felt the pain of Bob's explosive anger too. After Bob had convinced himself that Sandy was not his daughter, he treated her like a servant.

One day Bob told 4-year-old Sandy to fix him a sandwich while he watched a football game. Sandy struggled to get the items from the refrigerator and had to stand on a chair to reach the counter. As she worked on her father's sandwich, Bob burst into the kitchen and demanded to know where his sandwich was. Stunned by his outburst, Sandy stood frozen in fear. Bob lunged at Sandy and struck her several times across the face, shouting that she was stupid and lazy. He accused her of not listening to him and demanded that she tell him why she was being so naughty. Sandy couldn't open her mouth for fear of experiencing more of her father's anger. Bob then sat Sandy on the counter and proceeded to feed her teaspoons of Tabasco sauce to punish her for being disobedient and disrespectful to her father. He warned her never to tell her mother about this episode, telling her that that too would be disobedient and disrespectful, and that she would have to be punished again.

The family came to counseling when Michelle threatened to leave Bob. He had agreed to see a counselor but not to seek help for his problems. He wanted the therapist to help Michelle see how wrong it was for her to leave her husband. He continually reminded the therapist that his wife and *children were disobedient and disrespectful to him; they were subverting the authority that the Bible gave him to control his family.*

Michelle stayed with her husband even though the counseling failed to change his twisted perspective on life. Her response was characteristic of many nonabusive spouses—the guilt she felt for not protecting Sandy kept her from leaving Bob. And as an abused spouse she also felt that she was responsible for bringing the abuse on herself and her daughter.

A Living Hell

Victims of physical abuse live in the chaos and confusion of trying to obey the abuser's rigid and unreasonable demands. They soon learn that whether they are obedient or not, painful physical abuse still occurs. Fear of further harm keeps these victims from reporting the abuse; they suffer silently, trying to hide their bumps and bruises from others. Their actions reflect the great fear they have of the abuser as well as their belief that the abuse is, in part, their own fault.

Sadly, sometimes victims from abusive Christian families find it more difficult to report abuse than do victims from non-Christian families. Since discipline and restraint are usually seen as virtues in the church, these victims aren't sure that their church will support them. For such Christians, fear of being alienated from the church drives them to remain silent. The thought that the church might side with the abuser is so frightening that the victim may feel that he or she will be better off just trying to deal with it, as if the abuse is their "cross to bear" in life.

The Bible Tells Me So

Many perpetrators of physical abuse have found easy justification for their actions within the pages of the Bible. These people twist God's Word, figuring that their violent actions are part of God's will or that harsh discipline is part of their Christian responsibility. The following verses and their explanations provide examples of this way of thinking.

- Exodus 20:12. This verse provides perhaps the easiest justification for child abuse. If the child is not obedient, then this fifth commandment gives the abuser a good reason to be angry and to take the action that he or she takes. This same abuser may go on to describe his or her physical response as similar to God's retaliation against his sinful people in the Old Testament.

- Proverbs 13:24, 22:15, 23:13, 29:15. These proverbs extol the virtues of discipline—an obvious necessity—in child rearing. But physical abusers take this instruction too far. They may feel that if they do not respond with harsh physical discipline, then their children will grow up spoiled and undisciplined. And some abusers literally interpret the word *rod* to mean that they should use a rod or some other implement to discipline a child even when other, less violent techniques have been effective.

Sometimes such abuse is carried out in the name of Christian love. These verses from Proverbs can easily be interpreted to mean that if a parent doesn't discipline her child, she must not really love the child. Justifying harsh physical punishment in this way is extremely harmful to children and adults because it communicates to them that people are loving them when they are really hurting them. Many children who were abused this way often find themselves in abusive relationships as adults. They feel that in order to be truly loved, they must take a certain amount of abuse. Further, many of these adults follow the pattern that their abusive parents set years earlier when they deal with their own children. But harsh physical discipline does not equal love. Such behavior is a distortion of the love that God really intends to exist between family members.

- Ephesians 5:22. Abusive husbands have taken this verse out of context, interpreting it to mean that they have a responsibility to control their wives if they refuse to "submit." They feel that such refusal is considered contrary to God's will for marriage, and that abuse is necessary to bring the wife back to a biblical understanding of what her behavior ought to be.

- Matthew 18:21-22. After physical abuse has taken place, some abusers claim that the victim shouldn't report it. After all, they are supposed to forgive their fellow Christians not just seven times, but "seventy-seven times." (Jesus used this number to represent perfect forgiveness.) Abusers who have been asked to leave the family often point to this verse as an indicator that the *victim* is being unchristian because of his or her unwillingness to take the abuser back.

- Ephesians 6:1. In this verse we read that children are to obey their parents, because it is the right thing to do. A tragic situation develops when church leaders encourage children to obey their parents but are unaware that abuse is taking place in the home. These children grow up feeling confused over the Bible's teachings about obedience. How can a faith that promotes love also allow physical abuse to occur? This confusion leads children also to believe that God condones abuse. After all, the Bible is God's Word, and their parents use this book to justify their actions. Such children often become alienated from the church and from God in later years.

Marjorie's father served as an elder and a deacon in the family's church. He took his responsibility as head of the household very seriously, making sure that his children knew what solid "Christian discipline" was all about. After-dinner devotions around the kitchen table sometimes lasted for two hours or more as he read chapters of the Bible and interpreted them to the family. If any of the children showed signs of restlessness, Marjorie's father would start over again.

Marjorie recalled one incident when her father read and interpreted the Ten Commandments. When he came to the fifth commandment, he stopped and asked the children what sins they might have committed that their parents did not know about. The children around the table knew that if they denied any wrongdoing, their father would loudly accuse them of being liars. Marjorie said that as each child fearfully told one story, her father's face grew redder and angrier. As the last child shared some activity unknown to her father, Marjorie's dad leaped from the table and began to curse each of the children for being so bad and so worthless. He claimed he didn't know what he had ever done to deserve such rotten children.

For the rest of that evening, her father took his children one by one to the chicken coop, where he severely beat each child using a whip, a horse strap, and a board.

When Marjorie left her parents' house on her eighteenth birthday, never to return, she also left God's house. She was a very sullen and unhappy woman when she first came to the support group for abused women. Although she was married to a man who did not abuse her and who was devoted to his denomination, Marjorie still refused to attend church services. And when the abuse group chose to study forgiveness, Marjorie asked to be excused.

The Other Side of Physical Abuse

In our last session we learned that emotional abuse has two sides—spoken abuse and silence. In the same way, the physical abuse that we have discussed in this session also has a silent partner: neglect.

People hear and read about physical and sexual abuse, but the problem of neglect is not publicized nearly as often. And while the other three forms of abuse all have the word *abuse* in the label (physical abuse, sexual abuse, and emotional abuse), neglect is not similarly labeled. But it is no less a form of abuse than the others. In fact, neglect has some distinct similarities to emotional abuse.

First, neither neglect nor emotional abuse leaves physical bruises or injuries. Since there is no physical evidence, its effect on the victim is often unfairly diminished.

Second, because neither one receives the priority of the authorities, many victims of neglect and emotional abuse do not regard the behavior as abusive. Rarely is someone prosecuted for emotional abuse. Fortunately, neglect is prosecuted a little more often, but definitely not as often as it should be.

Third, the lower status of these two forms of abuse is reflected in the lack of treatment programs for victims and for offenders. In contrast, treatment programs for victims and perpetrators of physical and sexual abuse abound.

Neglect of the Young

Often people don't see neglect as abuse because it is associated with poverty and under-employability (that is, an individual's income obtained from working is so minimal that he or she cannot afford many necessities). Rather than hassle a family that is already having a difficult time, most people have a tendency to look the other way when neglect occurs. And in some of these situations, neglect occurs simply because the parents don't know what they need to provide for their child.

But sometimes neglect is intended to punish or harm a child. When a child is ignored, or when life's simple necessities are withheld because the child has been "bad," the child's self-esteem can be seriously damaged. Also, the trust relationship that is so necessary to the normal development of the parent/child relationship is betrayed. When such neglect occurs intermittently over a period of years as a form of punishment, a normal, trusting relationship can be difficult to salvage.

Neglect can also interfere with the child's development. Children do not perform as well in school when their physical needs are neglected. And neglect can instigate negative behaviors in children as they inappropriately crave attention from others, hoard or steal food, bully other children for their possessions, and, in later years, turn to chemicals to ease the pain.

Neglect of the Elderly

This serious situation warrants our special attention. Neglect of the elderly can include failing to provide needed medical care; over-medicating; withholding possessions as a form of punishment; withholding money that the individual is entitled to; failing to respond to an individual's pleas that he or she is being taken advantage of; and leaving an elderly person who can't care for him- or herself alone for a long period of time.

The elderly are neglected for many different reasons. Sometimes family members or caregivers become angry or frustrated with the demands of caring for them. Sometimes elderly people become so helpless that they seem like young children again. This angers and frustrates caregivers and family members who grow sick and tired of Mom or Dad's childish behavior. And sometimes an unresolved family matter can lead to neglect—the elderly person is punished for something that probably took place many years ago.

Unfortunately, neglect of elderly persons is often easy to accomplish. By virtue of their age or health, they have been judged by society as being powerless and weak. In this case the perpetrator either thinks that his parent can't complain, or that no one will believe her if she does.

Like children, elderly persons suffer the effects of being neglected. An elderly victim of neglect may fear his caregivers or family members, because he knows that complaints may result in even less care. At times, this fear can turn to anger as the elderly person becomes aware that the neglect is due to his age or limitations.

Guilt is also a common response to being neglected. An elderly victim of neglect may believe that she has done something earlier in life to deserve this kind of treatment. She experiences a deep sadness that comes from realizing that there is little she can do to change the situation. Depression is commonly associated with elderly persons who have been or are being neglected.

The Church's Response

Too many episodes of neglect take place behind closed doors, and victims suffer in silence. While the church cannot be in every home at every moment, it *can* help families avoid abusive situations. The church can choose to teach its members proper and healthy relationships as revealed in the Bible and exemplified in Jesus Christ. It can also provide support to families who are impoverished and to caregivers who grow weary of caring for children or elderly persons. Finally, the church should be seen as a place of healing and hope for the abused and the abusers, a place where they can look for a helping hand out of the destructive spiral of physical abuse and neglect.

Suggestions for Group Session

Getting Started

Begin by reading together Genesis 2:18-24, a passage that shows us the loving relationship God intended for husbands and wives. Emphasize that, just as spouses must be seen as a gift from God, so also other family members must be seen as God's gifts to us. Sing a song of your choosing, then ask one of your group members to open with prayer.

Group Discussion and Activity

From Chapter Three

1. What did the text say about the demands made by physical abusers?

2. How could Bob and Michelle and their children have benefitted from a support group?

From Your Experience

None of us enjoys hearing stories of abuse or neglect. Yet we must become aware of these incidents in our community so that we can give victims the serious consideration and support that they need. Encourage

37

each other to share stories about abuse or neglect that you have read or heard about recently.

1. Stories about abuse are reported to police and children's protective service workers every day. From reading these stories in the newspaper, why do you think children do not report crimes of physical abuse?

2. Children often pose difficult discipline issues for their parents. Some physical abuse comes as a result of the parents' frustration about not knowing how to handle these issues. What are some nonphysical alternatives to resolving these frustrating situations?

3. In one sentence, describe the benefits of providing support groups for victims of abuse. Do you know of any in your neighborhood or community? Could your church start a support group for physically abused persons?

From the Bible

Divide into two groups: all men in one and all women in the other. Find a separate place in the room to meet and talk quietly. Each group will read Ephesians 5:21-33 and 6:1-4, and will answer the following questions:

1. What does it mean for a wife to submit to her husband?

2. What does it mean for a husband to love his wife?

3. What does the second passage say about how parents should treat their children?

Come back together in the larger group and compare your answers. Then discuss the first two questions.

1. How has the church you attend historically viewed these verses? Discuss any problems that may have arisen because of those interpretations.

2. How does verse 33 resolve some of the differences?

Closing Prayer

In the chapter, Bob and Michelle lived together for a long time before Bob's abusive behavior showed itself. As a group, read aloud Ephesians 5:13 and then pray for the courage to confront the secret sins of abuse however and whenever they appear.

FOUR

THE UNSPOKEN SIN

People generally do not want to openly discuss the sin of sexual abuse, yet our study has shown its prevalence even among Christians.

- *Margie was the 26-year-old single parent of 4-year-old Katie. During bath time each week, Margie and Katie would share the bathtub for a shampoo and scrubbing. Following bath time, Margie would reward Katie for her good behavior in the bathtub by allowing her to touch Margie's breasts and genitals. To Katie the touching was a reward for good behavior; to Margie it provided sexual arousal.*

  When Katie shared stories of her bath time and reward with a day-care provider, Margie was reported to children's protective services. Margie appealed to her pastor for legal aid after she was charged with lewd behavior involving a child. The pastor agreed with Margie that no harm was done to Katie—at her age she was incapable of understanding what her mother found so pleasurable. Several church members supported Margie by attending her hearing and harassing the protective-services worker. After several months of legal battles financed by the church Margie attended, the prosecutor dropped the charges, realizing that Katie would not qualify as a witness against her mother.

- *After the end of a long day working the fields, Roy and his three teenage sons would return to the farmhouse for a dinner of meat and potatoes. While Roy's wife and daughter stayed in the house to tidy up, Roy and his sons headed out to the barn for one last check on the animals. Once inside the barn, Roy would pull out several pornographic magazines and a slide projector with a slide tray of nude women with male partners in various positions. After carefully hiding the magazines and projector, Roy and his sons would return to the house. Their purpose for returning to the barn each night had been kept a secret for several years.*

• *Jerry and Sara came to counseling after fifteen years of marriage. They said they weren't communicating with each other. Later Sara revealed that Jerry was demanding sexually and that she preferred to stay up until after Jerry had gone to bed to avoid him. Jerry, angered by her withdrawal of affection, became more aggressive. On one occasion, Jerry interrupted Sara's shower and dragged her into the bedroom where he forced intercourse with her. On another occasion, Jerry bound Sara's hands and feet before engaging in intercourse with her. Both times, Sara pleaded with Jerry to stop and cried in pain when Jerry forced himself on her.*

What Is Sexual Abuse?

Sexual abuse is intimacy that is forced upon another

• without their consent,
• without their knowledge,
• without their understanding of what is taking place, or
• without a means to resist and prevent the intimacy.

Sexual abuse can be both physical and nonphysical. Victims of sexual abuse can be of any age. The sexual abuser may be a stranger, but often the abuser is well known to the victim: a friend or neighbor, a relative living in the same household, or even a marriage partner.

Sexual abuse can take many forms. Some of these include

• obscene phone calls
• exposure of genitalia and breasts
• excessive hugging and kissing
• fondling body parts
• forced participation in the making of pornographic material
• forced viewing of pornographic material
• digital and penile penetration
• oral and anal sexual intercourse

In addition, sexual abusers may masturbate in the presence of minors or adults, grab the victim's breasts or buttocks, perform sex acts in the presence of minors, make obscene gestures, or use sexually explicit language in reference to their victims. All these acts and many others force unwanted intimacy upon another person. The word *force* implies that either the adult victim refuses to consent to the intimacy, or—in the case of a child or teenager—cannot legally give consent to the intimacy.

40

Sexual abuse is perpetrated against children, adolescents, and adults. The rest of this chapter will look more closely at sexual abuse in these three areas.

Child Sexual Abuse

Judy was the oldest of three girls in her family. When she was seven years old, her father invited her into his basement workshop to show her a toy box he was building. Her dad promised to give her the toy box if she would allow him to put his penis in her mouth. She agreed. The afternoon event was repeated several times a week, but Judy never got the toy box because her dad complained that Judy would not keep his penis in her mouth for very long. Judy tried to keep it in longer, but it made her sick and she couldn't.

When she finally told her dad she wasn't going to do it anymore, he told her that if she didn't, he would make her younger sister come downstairs, and he would put his penis in her mouth. Judy believed her dad and cooperated, thinking he would only expect this of her and would leave her sister alone. She continued to comply out of fear for her sister until she was 12 years old.

As an adult, Judy learned that her dad had lied. He had taken not one, but both of her younger sisters into the basement with the promise of receiving the toy box. He had abused each of his three daughters for approximately five years.

As in Judy's case, sexual abusers of children often threaten their victims so they will continue to comply and so that they will not report the abuse. These threats often involve the loss of a favorite toy or pet, harm to themselves or to another sibling, harm to the nonabusive parent, or the loss of privileges or physical necessities.

On the other hand, some sexually abused children are rewarded for their participation in the abuse. They are given a new toy, a new dress, a favorite candy, or a trip to the movies. In such cases the child assumes that the sexual activity is a good thing. The child may continue to participate as long as he or she continues to be rewarded.

Children may not report sexual abuse because they do not really understand what is going on. The abuse may continue for some time until the child either experiences physical pain or grows old enough to begin to understand the behavior as sexual and abusive. By that time, the child feels guilty for having participated for so long.

Oftentimes there is an element of trust in the relationship, especially if the abuser is a favorite relative or a parent. In order to maintain a good relationship during times when the abuse is not occurring, the child may choose not to say anything.

Even when they do tell, children are often not believed. They are accused of making up stories of abuse. Older children are sometimes punished for telling stories about abuse episodes and are angrily told not to say anything like that again.

The effects of sexual abuse on children are devastating. Abused children have a problem understanding what kinds of behavior are abusive. This confusion can later lead to difficulties in developing healthy relationships, in developing coping skills, and in protecting themselves. While the abuse continues, their self-esteem is at an all-time low.

Abuse may also seriously affect a child's spiritual development. Children who are taught in Sunday school to seek God in times of trouble feel that God has let them down by allowing the abuse to occur. God is supposed to love the child; then again, the abuser makes the same claim. How can a child distinguish between the earthly person who doesn't live up to his/her statements of love and the heavenly Father who is supposed to be a God of love?

An abused child may end up having difficulty believing in a loving, caring Father God. The child can learn to distrust all adults and even to distrust the church.

Adolescent Sexual Abuse

Carolyn was an adolescent victim of sexual abuse. Her father was a minister in a church in an upscale suburb that featured manicured lawns, housekeepers, and BMWs. Carolyn's abuse began when she was a 7-year-old. Her father insisted that she sit on his lap after supper and tell her the events at school that day. While Carolyn told her stories, her father massaged her crotch.

When Carolyn turned a little older, her father made the same request. Only now he asked her to come to his bedroom, and he reminded her to take her panties off before she came in. Carolyn was very fearful of and angry at her father. She promised herself over and over again that she would tell someone what her father was doing to her. Someone besides her mother, that is—she believed her mother knew what was happening and condoned it.

Finally Carolyn told a girlfriend's mother, who promised to help her. She notified the authorities, who came and removed Carolyn from the house until the details could be straightened out. Carolyn's mother and father were outraged at the accusations and banned Carolyn from contact with any of her family members, including her brothers and sisters. Her parents refused to visit a counselor because they claimed that the charges were preposterous.

Carolyn's father was charged and a trial date set. Carolyn told her story on the witness stand, and her father's attorney did everything he could to discredit her. The judge decided in the father's favor for lack of physical evidence.

Carolyn's father, who had been temporarily suspended from his duties, was reinstated. The high school where Carolyn attended refused to let her in after the trial was over. Carolyn's parents were told to pick their daughter up from the foster home, but they never showed up. Carolyn stayed at the foster home until she graduated from another high school. She was forbidden to see her siblings the entire time she was in foster care.

Carolyn's story is a tragic example of why teenage victims of sexual abuse have such a difficult time talking about their plight. Some of the reasons why such abuse goes unreported are outlined below.

• They experience guilt and shame, and do not want to make that guilt and shame public.

• Like children, they may also fear that their story will not be believed by adults.

• They, too, may be threatened by the perpetrator not to reveal the abuse.

• Because of their age, they may feel that they will be blamed for the abuse taking place. They feel like they should have been old enough to protest.

• They fear that they will be rejected by their friends and family if the adult successfully denies the abuse—especially if the abuser is a pastor, youth leader, a parent, or a relative.

• They fear that they will be responsible for dividing the family.

Some adolescent victims of sexual abuse have been accused of being provocative and promiscuous. This "blaming the victim" diminishes the guilt of the abuser and places the blame on the victim. Because of this, fewer adolescents come forth with their stories of abuse.

Some adolescents deny the abuse—even when it is occurring. Denial is one way in which some teenagers deal with the extreme physical and psychological pain and humiliation of abuse. But a problem as deeply harmful as sexual abuse can only stay hidden for so long. As a result of denial, some sexually abused adolescents may try to find comfort in drug or alcohol abuse—or even suicide.

Abused adolescents experience a reduced level of self-esteem and an inhibited ability to trust adults. In their social relationships they may suffer physical pain, anger, and frustration. And in much the same way as with abused children, an abused adolescent's spiritual growth and development may also be affected.

The sexual abuse of a teenager comes at a time when his or her sexual identity is just being formed. Abuse at such a time can throw the victim into despair and confusion regarding his or her sexual identity. As a result, the victim may have a difficult time in future years forming a sexually intimate relationship with a marriage partner. Such sexual abuse may also lead to homosexual behavior. Tragically, the confused adolescent victim may grow into an abuser him- or herself. Patterns of abuse have been shown to be born and recycled through generations.

Adult Sexual Abuse

Many people have difficulty accepting the fact that sexual abuse can occur between husband and wife. The church, for the most part, has also held to the notion that the activities between married persons ought to be considered private.

But sexual abuse between adults does not only take place on the marriage bed. Many college students and young adults are the victims of date rape and sexual violence. Many women also report incidences of sexual assault in grocery store parking lots, in beach bathhouses, and at parties.

Statistics show that 80 percent of abusers know their victims well. The remainder are perpetrators who stalk their victims or randomly pick them for assault. On the average, women report only 10 percent of the sexual assaults committed against them. And when the abuser is a spouse, that number dwindles to nearly zero.

Like children and adolescents, adult victims of abuse often do not report such abuse for fear that they will not be believed, or because they're afraid of being further victimized by the abuser. They experience the same guilt and shame as other abused people, and do not want to risk the public humiliation that goes along with being accused of letting it happen or, worse yet, "asking for it."

Married victims will not always report the abuse because they are attempting to keep the marriage together or to protect their children. The secret of the sexual abuse becomes a bargaining tool that more often than not becomes a weapon for the abuser—not the abused. Some married victims simply do not report abuse because they do not know where to turn for help or because they do not know what proper behavior within a marriage is. And some do not report the abuse because they believe that, over time, they can help the perpetrator stop his or her abusive behavior.

In many ways, the adult victim of sexual abuse goes through many of the same stages of frustration, humiliation, and denial as a child or an adolescent. But many adult victims feel trapped because they are married to the perpetrator. While children can be placed in another home and adolescents can run away, wives and husbands have entered into a binding agreement. Those who contemplate leaving the relationship have to deal with the spiritual, emotional, financial, social, and even physical consequences of their decision. These issues can be decidedly more complex if the abuser is the breadwinner and the victim-spouse is without financial resources.

Church leaders sometimes suggest that the abused partner stay in an abusive relationship. They will argue that the victim stay for the sake of the family, or because the abuse isn't bad enough to merit the spouse leaving. Victims who receive such advice from representatives of the church can despair of ever getting out of the abusive situation. Since they don't receive the care and compassion that they need at church, such victims may turn from their church and withdraw from their religious community.

Last Thoughts

It is clear from our study that the sins of abuse leave a terrible impact on the victims/survivors. These terrible effects are not diminished by time. The church and community must act quickly and with compassion to bring a halt to these crimes. The victims of abuse must be encouraged to drink deeply from the healing well that is Jesus Christ.

Suggestions for Group Session

Getting Started

For many people, sexual abuse is a difficult subject to confront and discuss. The incidents of sexual abuse reported in this study may make some group members uncomfortable, either because they can identify with the victims or because of the explicitness of the reporting. You may decide as a group to discuss this session in two groups—men in one group and women in the other.

Open your session with prayer, asking that God will give you courage to deal openly with this subject of sexual abuse. Then read together the following words from "Our World Belongs to God":

Since God made us male and female in his image,
one sex may not look down on the other,
nor should we flaunt our sexuality.
Our roles as men and women must conform
to God's gifts and commands
as we shape our cultural patterns.
Sexuality is disordered in our fallen world;
grief and loneliness are the result;
but Christ's renewing work gives hope
for order and healing
and surrounds suffering persons
with a compassionate community.

Group Discussion and Activity

From Chapter Four

1. What is sexual abuse?

2. The session cites many different examples of sexual abuse. Pick out one or two of the episodes and discuss what the long-term effects

might be for the victims and the perpetrators. (*Note:* Don't forget to discuss the issue of Roy and his sons.)

3. According to the author, what are some of the reasons why sexual abuse goes unreported?

4. How is self-esteem often affected by sexual abuse?

From Your Experience

1. Though it may be difficult, please share an example of sexual abuse that you have heard or read about recently.

2. If possible, share what some of the long-lasting effects have been in these cases.

From the Bible

Divide up into three groups. Each group will read a passage and respond to the questions. Then come back together into the larger group for reporting.

Group 1

Read 2 Samuel 13:1-22.

1. Amnon says in verse 4b that he's in love with his sister Tamar. After reading the story, do you think he loved her? How would a child or spouse feel after being sexually violated by someone who says that they love them?

2. What was Jonadab's role in this episode?

3. In verse 9, Amnon orders everyone to leave so he might be alone with Tamar. What does this suggest about perpetrators?

4. Who pays the greater price in verse 13?

5. How might a victim today respond to the rejection in verse 16?

6. What was Absalom's reaction and response? Put yourself in Absalom's position. Would you say or do anything differently to Tamar to comfort her?

7. Verse 21 suggests that this event was covered up for a time. When he heard about it, King David was furious. But it is evident from later verses that he didn't do much of anything after hearing of the rape. What should he have done? Why do you think he did nothing?

Group 2

Read 2 Samuel 13:1-22.

1. How might Tamar have felt when she was asked to bake bread for an ill relative?

2. How might Tamar have felt when Amnon grabbed her and demanded sex?

3. How might Tamar have felt after Amnon forced himself on her against her protests?

4. How might Tamar have felt after Amnon ordered her out of the room and she returned to her own quarters?

5. How might Tamar have felt about her brother Absalom and what he said?

6. How might Tamar have felt about herself after the rape?

Group 3
Read Ephesians 5:1-21.

1. What kinds of practices does Paul warn against in verses 3 and 4?

2. What does verse 6 say about perpetrators who try to excuse what they have done?

3. What does verse 7 say about how we should relate to these perpetrators?

4. According to verse 11, what does Paul suggest the Christian community do when it becomes aware of abuse?

5. How should we be living as Christians according to verses 1, 8, 15, 21? What does this say about our thoughts and actions?

After reporting on the results of your Bible studies, discuss what all of this means for you as members of a church (or churches). How could Ephesians 5:1-21 contribute to a policy or practice in your church community? Discuss in which areas of the church such policies or practices may be needed. How should you respond to abused persons? How can you help prevent abuse from occurring in your personal lives?

Closing Prayer
The church community knows many Tamars and many Amnons. Pray for justice and compassion for the Tamars and for wisdom in dealing with the Amnons. Pray too that the Lord might lead you to participate in a ministry to such people.

FIVE

AN INDIVIDUAL RESPONSE TO ABUSE

Steve and Hannah fought about the same things most young couples fight about. They fought over money, they argued over who was going to do what chores, and they both were adamant about whose family's house they would go to on Thanksgiving Day.

Steve liked to win these kinds of arguments. In fact, Steve liked to win every argument. When they fought, Hannah often cried about how unfair it was that Steve always got his way. This crying usually irritated Steve. One night, however, his anger got out of control—he slapped Hannah across the face. After this incident, Steve continued to lash out at Hannah. One evening he pushed her while they fought in the kitchen. Hannah lost her footing, fell, and knocked her head against the stove. A small trickle of blood came from a wound near her forehead. Hannah couldn't even muster a tear, and Steve looked away and went downstairs to work on a project. Later that night, Steve was exceptionally gentle and kind to Hannah. Did she want anything to drink or to snack on? Should he turn up the furnace a little more so she was warm?

Steve continued to abuse his spouse for many months. One night while Steve was out bowling, Hannah took her two children with her to the local police department. She asked for directions to a shelter for abused women. She was asked if she wanted to file charges against her husband, but she declined. She didn't want to get Steve in trouble with his boss.

Upon the advice of the women at the shelter, Hannah called home late that night to tell Steve she wasn't coming home until he got counseling and stopped abusing her. Steve's immediate reaction was one of intense anger.

49

Did she know how embarrassing this was for him? He insisted that she come home right away—before the neighbors started to talk. Finally they both hung up, unable to convince each other of what they wanted.

Every day Hannah called home. Every day Steve pleaded with her to come back. He agreed to treat her better and promised her that things would be different. Steve wanted to see his daughters, but that was against the shelter's policies. Steve accused Hannah of breaking up the family— they were his kids; he was entitled to see them. Hannah's pastor also contacted her during this time. He urged her to give Steve another chance; after all, Steve was a hard worker and a good provider. And he never hurt the kids, did he?

After seven days Hannah relented. She called Steve to say she and the kids would be coming home. Upon returning home, Hannah found a sink full of dirty dishes and laundry stacked sky high. Could she clean the place up and make some chip dip? He had invited some guys over to watch the basketball finals.

Kurt is a 36-year-old self-employed businessman. He owns a lumber company that he bought from a friend of his father when the economy slowed down in that area of the country. Because of excellent business skills, his business grew immensely. He was even given an award by his community's Chamber of Commerce because of his business acumen. His goal was to be a millionaire by age 35, and he succeeded.

Kurt is a deacon in the church he was baptized in and attended all his life. He also serves on several agency boards and was picked to be the chairperson of the finance committee to raise funds for the local Christian schools. To people at the church and at his work, he is the picture of a man who has it all together.

But there is a dark side to his success. Kurt has been physically abusive to his wife, Valerie, for three years. He has broken her jaw, dislocated a shoulder, and given her several black eyes, a swollen lip, and deep bruises on both of her arms.

Abuse Is All-Pervasive

If this were an ideal world, none of us would have to live in communities that are stained with the sin of abuse. Our churches would never have to reach out to broken and humiliated victims, nor would they ever have to confront abusers. But the sin of abuse exists in every community and among every body of believers. Every Sunday we knowingly or unknowingly worship with abuse victims and abusers. We participate in community events and in everyday activities with both victims and abusers. Even this course will be studied by both victims and perpetrators of abuse.

There is a purpose behind increasing the Christian community's awareness about the sin of abuse and its impact on victims. The Christian community needs to reach out to both victims and perpetrators. It needs to be seen as a place where help and healing can be found. Because of the all-pervasiveness of abuse, this book has a two-fold purpose: to increase the Christian community's awareness about matters of abuse and to help that community respond to abusers and victims.

Why Does Abuse Occur?

Abuse is about *power*. Regardless of whether or not the victim and the perpetrator know each other, every abusive situation or relationship contains some kind of an imbalance of power that results in abuse.

The quest for power will block out any sympathy the perpetrator may have toward the victim. However, once the perpetrator experiences the relief of being back in control, he or she may then express some remorse for the abusive behavior. Such wide mood swings with their accompanying promises can be very convincing to the victim, who may live in the hope that, *this time,* the perpetrator will keep his or her promise to stop the abuse. This kind of thinking traps victims into staying in abusive relationships. But promises to stop the abuse, along with the remorse and guilt that the abuser expresses, are likely to be nothing more than a smoke screen to appease the victim, to keep civil authorities from taking action, and to pacify therapists and other involved parties.

Alarmingly, surveys taken in prison settings and in treatment programs for perpetrators reveal that nearly 80 percent of male abusers were at one time victims of child abuse. Among female abusers the percentage of those who had been abused as children is even higher! The sense of powerlessness that they felt when they were abused was the reason most of them gave for abusing others.

Abusers often act abusively because of the role models they had as they grew up. In homes where abuse and domestic violence exist, children are taught that there are basically two kinds of people: those who take abuse and those who dish it out.

Some abusers act the way they do because their culture rewards aggressive behavior. Teens often gain admittance to gangs only after they have committed an act of violence against another person. And let's not forget our own business environment, where raises, promotions, and bonuses are offered to employees who aggressively acquire accounts or upstage other employees for the boss's approval. An aggressive business attitude can translate into an aggressive attitude in other areas of life.

For some people, abuse is the only way to overcome a sense of hopelessness. People who have been laid off or fired from their jobs have traditionally been at high risk for behaving abusively. People who feel trapped by poverty, by long-standing unemployment, or by a job that barely allows the family to make ends meet tend to live under continual stress. These situations rob people of self-esteem, self-confidence, and security. Sometimes the only way individuals in these situations feel they can regain their lost sense of control is by physically or sexually dominating another person.

There are many other reasons why people abuse others; and sometimes people abuse for no reason at all. The preceding examples and descriptions are not intended to be exhaustive. They are only intended to help us understand the causes of abuse. If we can begin to understand why a person abuses, then we will begin to realize that the perpetrator will not stop on his own. He or she needs counseling and perhaps incarceration. Understanding the roots of abuse also forces us to acknowledge that the victim is not at fault and probably could have done nothing to prevent the abuse.

Profile of an Abuser

Abusers come in all shapes and sizes, from all socioeconomic levels, and from all races, creeds, and ethnic backgrounds. Abusers are found in both the broader community and in the church. Therefore, no one profile fits all. But there are some things that most abusers have in common:

- They may be loners—they like seclusion to carry out the abuse.

- They would rather spend time with children than adults.

- They find occasions to be alone with children, to play with children, and often act like children.

- They may have a history of being abused.

- They may have a history of abusing animals.

- They may focus attention on one child in a family to the exclusion of the other children.

- When accused of an abusive act, they often act surprised rather than hurt or angry. Being caught by another party is much worse than having to face your victim.

- They have difficulty respecting other people's privacy and personal space. They may brush up against others or "inadvertently" slide their hand against another's breast or buttocks.

- They like to be in control and to have things done their way.

- Most perpetrators begin with emotional abuse and progress to physical and sexual abuse. Often the first signs of emotional abuse point to the possibility of other forms of abuse being carried out.

Advice to Children

Everyone must learn how to avoid becoming another abuse statistic—and young children in particular. Following are four simple steps that teachers and parents should keep in mind when talking to children about abuse.

52

STOP!

When someone hurts them physically or sexually, they can and should say *STOP!* in their loudest voice. Most children are conditioned to do this when the offender is a peer or an older brother or sister. They have not been taught, however, that it is O.K. to tell a stranger or a familiar adult to *STOP!*

GO!

If someone tries to hurt them, or asks them to do something that they feel is inappropriate, they should *GO* away from that person as quickly as possible. If they are in a neighbor's house, they should run home. If they are in their own home, they should run to a neighbor's house.

TELL!

If another person has tried to hurt them or has in fact already hurt them, they should tell someone immediately.

TELL AGAIN!

Teach children that they may have to tell the story several times until someone believes them. But emphasize that they *must* tell—no matter what the people say who don't believe them.

Advice to Teens and Young Adults

Teens and single adults often date people whom they don't know very well. The immediate rush of excitement about being asked out should not cover over the fact that they need to learn as much as they can about the person they intend to date. If possible, they should talk to someone who knows that person well or who may have already dated that person.

If, after a few dates, the teen or young adult finds him- or herself in an abusive situation, the individual should act quickly to get out of the relationship. Sometimes teens or single adults date another person believing that they can change that person. This rarely works, even under the best of circumstances. It works even less when the behavior they are trying to change is abusive.

Sometimes teens or single adults who ask about their prospective dates think that they will be the exception—"Just because Tom treated others this way doesn't mean he'll treat me the same." The truth is, abusers often don't discriminate. The teen or adult who ignores the advice of someone who knows the other person well could be setting herself up for a very painful situation.

People don't often like to share what they know about another person with others. Such behavior could be seen as gossiping or spreading rumor, and it could reflect poorly on the teller. But if someone comes to you looking for information on another person, you need to consider it your responsibility to share any information that the other person may need to know. You could be preventing a friend from suffering at the hands of an abuser. If you don't tell, you could be leading the other person right into an abusive trap.

If someone comes to you with concerns about a friendship or about a friend who may be abusive, you should affirm that person and reassure him that you are taking him seriously. Any attempt to diminish his concerns or explain away the behavior may result in that person being put at risk of further abuse. Often someone who *thinks* they might be in a bad relationship is indeed *in* one.

Like children, teens or adults should feel free to say no to anything they feel is wrong. They should also observe carefully how their partner responds to such rejection. Anger and resentment are red flags that their rights and preferences may not be acceptable to the partner. While no one can be expected to hear no and really enjoy it, a nonabusive person in a relationship can tolerate different needs at different times with different outcomes.

Teens and adults who have survived childhood abuse should look for counseling. Many survivors of abuse find themselves in abusive situations as teens or adults. Survivors who undergo treatment with competent therapists can learn how their relationships have been affected by the childhood abuse. Once they recognize the facts behind the abuse, they can move on to healing and forgiveness. Dealing with the anger, guilt, and pain of child abuse in therapy helps teenagers and young adults make wiser choices about friends, employers, and lifetime mates.

Teens and adults need to recognize that under no circumstances should they stay in an abusive situation. Things will *not* get better. Nothing they begin doing or stop doing is likely to have a positive impact on the abuser. The situation will only get better if the abuser decides that he or she needs help to become better. If the victim chooses to stay in the relationship, the abuser may never come to that realization.

Finally, teenage and adult victims need to find support groups—either within a church setting, or within a community program. The church can often provide positive role models of relationships between men and women, young and old, peers, or even of those in authority and those under authority. Church and community support groups can also provide opportunities for victims to foster friendships with people who share positive relationship values like trust, fidelity, honor, respect, and mutual concern.

An Individual Response to the Abused

In the next chapter we will look at the community of believers and how it ought to respond to both victims and perpetrators. The remainder of this session will look at how we as individuals can respond to hurting people who come to us for help.

- *Affirm the survivor.* Survivors have often been told by their abusers that no one will believe them. This is especially true when the victim is a child and the perpetrator is an adult. The starting point on a journey of healing for survivors is with the first person who affirms them. Every time the survivor tells his or her story and is affirmed, he or she takes a significant step along the journey.

- *Recognize the signs of abuse.* To the untrained eye the signs of abuse may not be very obvious. Sometimes competent professionals need to be called in to recognize old scars, bruises, welts, vaginal lacerations, and hand prints as signs of physical or sexual abuse. The first signs that you need to recognize are *verbal.* If a child describes sexual behavior that would otherwise be beyond his or her comprehension and experience, you may assume that the child knows about those matters because he or she has witnessed them or has been victimized.

- *Notify the authorities when dealing with child abuse.* Call your local child-protection agency immediately if you suspect that abuse is taking place. After you make the initial call, it is their responsibility to investigate any complaints the child has and to substantiate them. When a child comes to you with a story of abuse, it is important that you tell the child what steps you will take and explain that you will take these steps out of concern for the child.

- *Encourage survivors to seek the help of a competent therapist.* Pastors, church leaders, family members, and friends all have a role to play in the healing process, but actual therapy is usually beyond their expertise. The therapist is someone who will be the sole advocate of the survivor. The advantage that the therapist has over other friends or relatives is objectivity—he or she maintains an objective role in the healing process, and the survivor can trust the feedback that they hear about their behavior and feelings.

- *Maintain confidentiality.* The story belongs to the survivor, and no one has the right to share it (except for when you contact the proper authorities in the case of child abuse). The survivor places great trust in you by sharing the story, and you must never violate that trust. If the victim needs to tell the story to someone else, he or she will make that decision; your responsibility is to respect the victim's privacy and to work quietly to ensure that both the victim and the perpetrator get the professional help they need. If you must share the story for some reason, obtain either verbal or written permission from the survivor, and be specific about what you need to share and why.

By following these steps, you can provide the victim with the immediate affirmation that is so necessary to beginning the journey to healing. The care and concern that you show to a victim could be the turning point in that person's life.

A Story of Healing

"It's so hard," Gayle says. "All the 'little girl' inside me wants to do is go under the basement stairs and hide." Gayle begins many of her counseling sessions by describing her childhood feelings of wanting to escape and hide from the awful wrath of her father. After four years of therapy, Gayle expresses this familiar sentiment each time life throws her a curve ball that she is not sure she can handle. She remembers being a little girl of seven and spending hours hiding under the basement stairs until either her father calmed down, or until she heard the ugly sounds of her mother being beaten—which meant that this time the kids were spared.

Gayle recalls that during her childhood her father became violent two to three times per week. Ironically, she remembers one three-year period when her father's outbursts were sharply curtailed—the years he served on the school board. She said her father boasted to the family that he had to maintain an image, and that they should thank him for tolerating their misbehavior while he went off to another meeting.

Neither of her parents have ever told Gayle that they love her. They did not attend her high school graduation or her nursing school graduation because they said she never did anything to make them proud of her. Due to the lack of her parents' approval or affirmation of her skills and talents, Gayle developed a compulsive hand-washing behavior that they mocked openly. No matter what she did, Gayle could never seem to impress her parents.

Gayle met Josh when they were both 22 years old. They got engaged after a six-week whirlwind romance. Gayle's mother and father liked Josh very much—so much that they told him that he was a special guy who didn't deserve to have to live with someone like their daughter. Gayle remembers her dad offering Josh money to elope so Josh didn't have to publicly tell the world that he loved Gayle. The whirlwind romance ended on the evening of their wedding when Josh physically assaulted Gayle in the hotel room. Gayle hid in the bathroom the rest of her wedding night while Josh slept fitfully on the bed.

Their marriage lasted eighteen months. Gayle's parents were furious when she requested to come back home. Gayle's father said that she was an embarrassment to him and that no man would want anything to do with her now. He cursed her for being childless after so many months of marriage, and he told her to her face that she probably wasn't a real woman anyhow.

Gayle began therapy after a failed suicide attempt brought her to her senses. During the first six weeks of therapy she chatted nervously about her work, her feelings of embarrassment about "the attempt," and her upcoming vacation plans.

Three months into therapy, Gayle was talking nonstop about her failed marriage and the feelings of anger she had toward her ex-husband. But she still had not admitted to the therapist that her ex-husband had abused her, or that her childhood had been a nightmare of physical abuse.

One day Gayle came to therapy announcing that her church had called a new pastor and that she had met him. "He seems so sensitive and caring," Gayle said. She went on to say that he was interested in hearing about her divorce, and that he had expressed remorse for the "wasted" time that she spent with Josh when she could have been in love with the "right" man. Gayle liked what her pastor had to say and began to visit with him more often. Occasionally, Gayle skipped her counseling sessions to meet with her pastor.

After a year of therapy, Gayle had changed dramatically—for the worse. She came to counseling only sporadically; when she came, she was always angry. She directed a lot of her anger at the therapist. When her therapist asked her questions about her anger, Gayle became defensive and sarcastic. The therapist assured Gayle that she would stick by her commitment to walk into unfamiliar hills and valleys with Gayle. She reassured Gayle that she could trust her implicitly.

Several months later, the therapist read that Gayle's pastor was preaching his farewell address that Sunday morning. Feeling that his departure was suspiciously sudden, the therapist feared the worst. Gayle canceled two appointments before finally coming in looking depressed, haggard, and unkempt. "I've been hiding underneath the stairs again," she said in the voice of a child expecting to be scolded. The therapist asked, "What happened?" And Gayle let loose with a deluge of tears and sobs that continued for two and one-half hours. Out came the childhood abuse, out came the spouse abuse, out came the abuse by her pastor. Through Gayle's tears the therapist was able to see through to the root of her client's pain. Gayle's emotions poured out like her tears: afraid, disgraced, hurt, dirty, humiliated, unloved, angry, lost, confused, betrayed.

Gayle's pastor was relieved of his duties by the regional church authorities. Although Gayle was asked to testify against him, she chose not to. Two other women did, however, and he was discharged from serving in the church. Gayle stayed away from the church for over a year after news of his abusive practices spread throughout the congregation.

Gayle continued individual therapy. She never missed an appointment. During these meetings, she learned to get to know that terrified child who hid under the stairs, and she was challenged to comfort that child and be a good parent to her. Most important of all, Gayle was not to allow that little girl to hide in the basement anymore. One day Gayle proudly announced that, though she had gone through a two-hour battle, she had stopped that child inside from hiding in the basement!

During the past two years, Gayle has not been to her parent's home, nor does she call them. She maintains contact with her family through a sister. Gayle's work has greatly improved—she has received a promotion as well as a commendation. While it is still hard for Gayle to accept compliments, her therapist has encouraged her to place her awards and cards of congratulations where she can see them every day to remind her of her importance and to bolster her self-worth.

Gayle began to attend a different church after being invited to a support group there. There Gayle learned that she was not at all alone—many other women had suffered the same kind of devastating abuse as children. The other women helped Gayle to see that the abuse distorted their sense of self and affected their view of what they needed as adults. Several of the group members acknowledged that they, too, had tolerated life in abusive marriages because they thought such activity was normal— they had come to expect it of their mates.

During one of the meetings, one young woman was overcome by grief as she recounted what she had lost as a result of the abuse she experienced. She got on her hands and knees and began to pray to God to help her. Several women reacted by joining her on the floor and hugging and consoling her. Gayle recounted the experience to her therapist, describing it as a real turning point for her. "While I was sitting around trying to blame God for the whole mess I was in, here was this lady asking him for help. I thought she was nuts until I saw how everybody responded to her. God really met her need right away. Something clicked in me, and I decided that God deserved another chance. The funny thing is that once I started to go back to church, it seemed like every sermon had a message geared directly for me."

And Gayle's new church was extremely supportive. Her paster met with Gayle and her therapist to see what more the church could do for her. He listened to her story, affirmed her, and assured her that her new church home would be a place where she could count on consistency and caring. He encouraged her to stay in therapy and offered his help when she needed it. Although only the therapist could hear it, Gayle's sigh of relief was deafening.

Because Gayle was willing to undergo therapy and join a support group, she was able to experience a measure of healing. By following the advice in this chapter, perhaps you could start a person like Gayle on the road to healing and health.

Suggestions for Group Session

Getting Started
Group members can join together in confessing these words from "Our World Belongs to God":

Apart from grace
we prove every day
that we are guilty sinners.
Fallen in that first sin,
we fail to thank God,
we break his laws,
we ignore our tasks.
Looking for life without God, we find only death;
grasping for freedom outside his law,
we trap ourselves in Satan's snares;
pursuing pleasure, we lose the gift of joy.
When humans no longer show God's image,
all creation suffers.
We abuse the creation or we idolize it.
We are estranged from our Creator,
from our neighbor, and from all that God has made.

Several group members should open with prayer, asking God to help each person present to show compassion not only for victims but also for the abusers. Pray that God will help the members of your group find helpful and appropriate ways to respond to abuse.

Group Discussion and Activity

Group members should do the exercises they feel will be most appropriate for the time allotted.

From Chapter Five

1. What do you think should have happened the night Steve first struck Hannah?

2. Why did Steve plead with his wife to return?

3. If Hannah were your daughter or friend, what advice would you give her?

4. Could spouse abuse ever warrant a marital separation? A divorce? Explain.

5. What was the difference between Steve and Kurt?

6. If both of their abusive stories were reported, how might Steve and Kurt be treated differently?

7. Counseling and incarceration are two treatment options for abusers that were mentioned briefly in this chapter. These two approaches are obviously quite different. Discuss the pros and cons of each approach and why you might recommend either one. Are there other approaches you would try? Explain.

From Your Experience

1. How open do you feel people are to sharing their stories of abuse?

2. Do you remember the first time you heard of an abusive situation? Did it involve a family member? A friend? A stranger?

3. If you have experienced abuse firsthand, or if you've read or heard about an abusive situation, what role did the balance of power play in it?

4. This chapter presents several suggestions for preventing abuse. How helpful do you feel these suggestions are? Can you think of other suggestions you might add?

From the Bible

Luke 23:34 reveals the compassionate spirit that Jesus had when he granted forgiveness to those who were crucifying him: "Father, forgive them, for they do not know what they are doing."

1. Discuss any stories that you've heard of where the abuser and the victim have been able to heal their relationship.

2. Do you think victims *have* to forgive their perpetrators? Explain.

3. What signs might indicate to a victim that the perpetrator is truly sorry for his or her abusive actions?

Closing Prayer

Because we all have sinned, we are all in need of God's gracious forgiveness. Pray that the Lord will forgive us for those sins we have committed against God and against others. Pray also that the abusers you've talked and heard about during your meeting might truly feel the Spirit convicting them of their sin, and that they might experience a contrite heart and seek the forgiveness of their victim(s).

SIX

A COMMUNITY RESPONSE TO ABUSE

Nancy is a 13-year-old middle school student. She is on the school honor roll and plays flute in the band. When her parents go out on occasional dates, Nancy is the designated baby-sitter for her three younger siblings.

One night when Nancy was baby-sitting, she started getting her siblings ready for bed. While her 18-month-old brother Jake was on the changing table, Nancy noticed the wrinkled skin of his testicles. She looked more closely and decided to touch the skin to see what it felt like. Her curiosity satisfied, she diapered Jake placed him in bed. Did Nancy sexually abuse Jake?

Lynda's father-in-law stops over most Sunday afternoons for a home-cooked meal and some play time with his grandchildren, Matt and Emily. Grandpa lives alone since his wife died, and Lynda thinks it's great that he feels welcome to come over and spend time with the family.

Grandpa usually gets tired about midafternoon. One afternoon he invited 7-year-old Emily to take a nap with him. Lynda was embarrassed by her daughter's refusal and insisted that Emily take a nap. With Grandpa still in his Sunday clothes and Emily in her play clothes, Grandpa cuddled with Emily on her bed and stroked her hair. He told her how pretty she was and how much he loved her. Then Grandpa told Emily that she shouldn't tell anyone how much Grandpa loved her because it would make her brother Matt jealous. He told her that it would be just their little secret. Did Grandpa abuse Emily?

A young man outraged his father by getting his ear pierced. His father struck him across the face with an open hand, giving the teenager a cut lip and an abrasion on his cheek. The youth pastor of their church was called in, and he met with the family for two hours. The father felt remorse for striking his son. The son acknowledged that he knew his decision to pierce his ear would antagonize his father, and he apologized to his father and mother. For the future, they promised to try to keep the lines of communication open. Do you think the son was abused?

These three cases remind us that the sin of abuse is not always easy to distinguish. They also point out how close we have all come to abusing someone we love. When abuse really does occur, the church needs to be there to respond in a positive way. This final chapter deals with the proper response the Christian community should have to the sin of abuse.

The Strengths of the Church

As we have seen, abuse is all-pervasive and very destructive. The whole matter of abuse might be too great for either victim or offender to deal with without some kind of support. The church can be very helpful in times of abuse if it knows how to respond. As an organization, the church has certain strengths that allow it to be an extremely positive support in such times.

Sheer Size and Numbers

The church involves a sizeable number of people in any given community. If church leaders make responding to abuse one of their mission goals, the church can serve to educate and support its members and other hurting individuals in its community. Many people can potentially be spared the trauma of abuse when the church becomes a place where children, teenagers, and adults are taught how to protect themselves or to get help for themselves. Because of the diverse programming opportunities that the church offers, every age group can be included in abuse education, and the message can be taught every few years.

Diverse Membership

Churches bring together people with a broad range of talents, abilities, and community influence. Within most churches there are members who can impact how the church responds to abuse—from those who can set up a system for reporting abuse, to those who can set up treatment opportunities, to those who can potentially change the legal system so that it better responds to abuse. In some communities, the church population is a sizeable majority of the citizens. That represents a powerful lobbying group if changes need to be made in the manner in which victims or abusers are handled.

Advocate for Family Values

The church supports family values and passes these on from generation to generation. It also fights against the disintegration of the family unit in the larger community. When the church becomes the advocate of the abused, it is seen as a secure and welcome haven for victims in a community that is often devoid of compassion and moral standards.

A Place of Healing

The church is a place where a person can find healing. Ideally, the church consists of compassionate, loving, gentle, and caring people. It ought to be one of the first places a person turns to when dealing with the effects of abuse or the awareness of being an abuser.

Bible-believing churches have all the tools they need to develop, maintain, and restore wholesome relationships between family and church members. These churches have the solid Word of God on which to depend for healing when healing is needed and for forgiveness when forgiveness is needed. Our God is a God of hope.

The Church's Response

The Christian community has a critical task in learning how to respond to victims and abusers. Like doctors and nurses in a medical emergency ward, the church must be prepared to deal with the crisis of abuse *before* the crisis actually occurs.

Churches need to build critical care units right within their own walls. Members who do the crisis intervention, however, must agree to two conditions: to do no additional harm to the victim, and to do everything in their power to bring the abused *and* the abuser to healing. The following items outline a blueprint for a church's basic response to abuse:

- *Acknowledge abuse from the pulpit.* Church members need to hear that the church leadership recognizes the sin of abuse and acknowledges that it exists even within the church community.

- *Educate about abuse.* While the church works to try to ease the pain that victims of abuse experience, it can't waste a moment in educating others on how to avoid abuse or how to avoid becoming an abuser. Education and prevention materials need to be made available to every grade, class, and society within the church—and to the community at large. Abuse experts and therapists need to address congregations, community leaders, and school personnel about abuse and its impact on victims.

  Such education again reaffirms abuse survivors. It tells them that what happened to them was wrong, that others recognize the terrible effect the abuse had on them, and that others care about them and want to see them healed. Such education also places the responsibility on the perpetrator, where it most appropriately belongs.

- *Develop policies to protect members and procedures to respond to abusers.* It is very important for a church to have policies in place regarding abuse. Such policies and procedures

  — communicate that the church will not tolerate abuse,
  — convey a proactive rather than a reactive response to abuse,
  — place an emphasis on healthy relationships, and
  — provide expectations within relationships that promote healing among survivors and perpetrators.

It is very important that a lawyer review any policy for dealing with abuse that a church may establish. A policy that seeks to deal with perpetrators must conform to the law and cannot deny a person his/her rights without due process. (One church's sample policy is included in the Appendix for your information.)

The Wrong Response

Many abused persons have been revictimized by well-intentioned persons who fail to understand how best to respond. Crisis interveners need to recognize that many perpetrators of abuse were at one time victims, and that they may have their own victimization to deal with. A well-intentioned (but poorly trained) friend could not only revictimize the abuser, but could also contribute to his or her denial of the abuse as well.

Sometimes within a church situation, crisis interveners try to bring the victim to the point of forgiving the abuser before everything has been worked through. If a victim is asked to forgive prematurely, he or she will not have grown sufficiently through the healing process to be able to forgive or to come out of the experience whole. Seeking an end to a painful chapter in a person's life, a crisis intervener may advocate that the victim forgive and try to forget. But so much may have been left unsaid or not dealt with. For the sake of both the abused and the abuser, sufficient time must be given before true healing and forgiveness can occur. And personal forgiveness does not necessarily exempt the abuser from legal prosecution.

Establishing policies and procedures for dealing with abuse will sometimes help prevent the church from responding the wrong way.

The Correct Response

There are many positive ways that the church can and should respond to victims of abuse.

- *Affirm victims and assure them that the church will be a place of healing for them.* These people need to know that the church understands. By acknowledging abuse and affirming the victims, church members become aware that they will be heard and affirmed.

- *Open the doors to an abuse support group.* The church community could offer the church building for such meetings and could even underwrite the cost of a therapist to lead the group.

- *Commit to walking through the whole healing journey.* Don't simply respond with empathy initially and then leave the victim stranded. Responding to abusive situations takes time and patience. Survivors need to know that they can come to the church throughout their healing journey for love, support, and encouragement.

- *Respond in a practical way.* Many crises occur on the healing journey. Whatever the crisis, the survivor needs to experience the security of a responsive community. Without prying, ask the survivor how he or she is doing. Offer support with meals, a lunch break, or child care to give a parent some time away. Tell the survivor you are praying for him or her. The Christian community may need to offer financial support, and may even need to provide safe shelter. Survivors in a Christian community ought to be embraced and welcomed, not isolated or treated as if they are contaminated.

Again, having policies and procedures in place will facilitate a positive and healthy response by the church community when an abuse situation becomes known.

Responding to the Abuser
The church needs to become a place of healing for the perpetrator of abuse as well as the victim. The following items outline how a church can effectively accomplish that goal.

- *Affirm the abuser's own history of abuse.* As we have read, abusers have often been victims of abuse themselves. When this is the case, the community needs to affirm those stories. The pain and anger of their own abuse is often buried deep within them and may not be easily reached.

- *Suggest professional counseling for the abuser.* A perpetrator's family members and church community ought not to accept an abuser back into the family or into active participation in the life of the church until a professional counselor indicates that it is safe and advisable to do so.

- *Set realistic expectations.* Just as a family has expectations about the behavior of its members, so the church can have expectations about its members and leaders. The church community is justified in asking an alleged perpetrator to refrain from attending services, or asking him or her to leave a paid position or office of the church for the safety and the sake of the other members. If the alleged statements are substantiated, the church community needs to separate the abuser from public church life until treatment is successfully completed.

- *Allow the legal authorities to do the investigating.* For the protection of all parties concerned, investigation of any allegation of abuse needs to be directed to legal authorities. It is their responsibility to investigate such matters. They have the authority, the experience, and the proper training to conduct such investigations.

- *Maintain appropriate contact with the abuser.* A delegation of trained members should meet with the perpetrator to support his or her needs for legal aid, financial aid, counseling referral, and spiritual encouragement. This delegation should serve as a liaison between the perpetrator and the church while the investigation is underway. If the investigation results in substantiated charges, this delegation ought to continue their role of offering support services to the perpetrator while a therapist or legal advisor helps them to monitor the abuser's progress toward healing.

Last Thoughts

The church can be a healing group for victims of abuse and for perpetrators. Too often the church has not reacted positively toward either. Through an understanding of abuse and its causes, the church can make the difference in the lives of both victims and perpetrators. Established policies and procedures will facilitate the healing process.

Suggestions for Group Session

Getting Started

Begin your session reading together the following words from the Contemporary Testimony:

The church is the fellowship of those
who confess Jesus as Lord.
She is the Bride of Christ,
his chosen partner,
loved by Jesus and loving him;
dclighting In his presence,
seeking him in prayer,
silent before the mystery of his love.

Pray for a willingness to make your church a place of healing for those who have experienced abuse. Pray that God will make clear to your group how your church can best meet the particular needs of both abused and abuser.

Group Discussion and Activity

There are more activities listed below than your group can probably address in one meeting. We suggest that the exercise on developing policies and procedures is crucial. If your church does not have such policies and procedures, you should seriously consider writing and adopting some. Consider meeting again if you don't have time to get to the policies exercise in this meeting.

From Chapter Six

1. Which suggestions regarding how the church should respond to abused persons were new to you?

2. What additional suggestions do you have for how the church should respond to abusers?

3. Review the specific suggestions about what the church could do regarding abuse in general, and discuss how they could be implemented in your situation.

From Your Experience

1. Has your church community been involved in an abuse case? If so, how did the church respond?

2. How could your church have responded?

3. How did individuals in your church respond?

From the Bible
    Read Luke 9:47-48.

1. Whom does Jesus choose to protect in this passage?

2. Why would Jesus be particularly concerned about these people?

3. How important is it to Jesus that we demonstrate love and concern for others?

    Read Luke 10:25-36.

1. What was the attitude of the first two people who came across the injured man at the side of the road?

2. What did the Samaritan do?

3. Jesus tells this parable to show us who our neighbors are. What should be our attitude toward our hurting neighbors?

4. What does this story have to do with abuse? How can we respond to the people who come to us needing our help?

Developing a Policy

The Appendix contains the abuse policies of one particular church. Read through these policies before going on to the questions below.

1. What is your church's current policy for responding to abused persons?

2. What is your church's current policy for responding to abusers?

3. What does your church teach children about avoiding becoming a victim of abuse?

4. Name the leadership positions in your church for whom policies and practices ought to be developed to protect the church from possible abuse situations.

Policies and procedures need to address the needs of the victims as well as the protection of the other members. You will not be able to develop a well-thought-out policy in a matter of hours. But if your church does not have a policy in place, you need to begin thinking about it. Before you leave your session today, set meeting dates for working on such a policy. If you do have a policy, you may want to review it closely to examine areas in which it can be improved.

Closing Prayer

Offer praise to God that we are not in bondage to our sin, but that if we confess it, he is sure to forgive us. Offer praise to Christ that there is healing for the brokenhearted. Offer praise for the Holy Spirit's vigilant walk with us as we seek to live wholesome lives within our families and community. And finally, thank God for making the church a community of caring Christian brothers and sisters.

APPENDIX

Audiovisual Resources

Videocassette Resources

Hear Their Cries (1991) and *Not In My Church* (1992). Center for the Prevention of Sexual and Domestic Violence, 1914 North 34th Street, Suite 105, Seattle, WA 98103.

Wake Up. Bethany Productions (1992). Bethany Christian Services, 901 Eastern Avenue NE, Grand Rapids, MI 49503.

The following videocassettes are available through TRAVARCA, the audiovisual lending library serving the Christian Reformed Church in North America (CRC) and the Reformed Church in America (RCA). For more information on any of these videocassettes, contact TRAVARCA at 4500-60th Street SE, Grand Rapids, MI 49512 (1-800-968-7221).

But Names Can Hurt Forever
Elder Abuse: Five Case Studies
Hear Their Cries: Religious Responses to Child Abuse
Listen to the Children
Picking up the Pieces
Ripped Down the Middle
To a Safer Place
Violence in the Home: Living in Fear
Why, God—Why Me?

Books

Battered into Submission. James Alsdurf and Phyllis Alsdurf. Downers Grove, IL: InterVarsity Press (1989).

Bold Love. Dr. Dan B. Allender. Colorado Springs, CO: NAVPRESS (1992).

Broken Boundaries: Resources for Pastoring People. Akron, PA: The Mennonite Central Committee Domestic Violence Task Force (1989).

Child Sexual Abuse: A Handbook for Clergy and Church Members. W. Carlson. Valley Forge, PA: Pilgrim Press (1988).

Helping Victims of Sexual Abuse. Lynn Heitritter and Jeanette Vought. Minneapolis, MN: Bethany House Publishers (1989).

How Can I Help Her? A Handbook for Partners of Women Sexually Abused as Children. Joan Spear. Center City, MN: Hazelden Press (1991).

Is Nothing Sacred? When Sex Invades the Pastoral Relationship. Marie M. Fortune. San Francisco, CA: Harper and Row (1989).

Lord, Heal My Hurts. Kay Arthur. Chattanooga, TN: Precept Ministries (1992).

Recovering from Sexual Abuse and Incest. Jean Gust and Patricia D. Sweeting. Bedford, MA: Mills and Sanderson (1992).

The Gift of Honor. Gary Smalley and John Trent. Nashville, TN: Thomas Nelson Press (1987).

The Mother's Book: How to Survive the Incest of Your Child. Carolyn M. Byerly. Dubuque, IA: Kendall/Hunt Publishing (1985).

The Purple Packet: Domestic Violence Resources for Pastoring People. Akron, PA: The Mennonite Central Committee Domestic Violence Task Force (1989).

Through the Tears: Caring for the Sexually Abused Child. Karen Cecilia Johnson. Nashville, TN: Broadman Press (1993).

Guidelines for All Church Members

The following guidelines are excerpted from the study committee report on abuse (Report 30) presented to the 1992 Synod of the Christian Reformed Church in North America. For a full copy of the report, see the *Agenda for Synod 1992*.

Members of the committee were:
Leonard D. Blaukamp
Peter Nicolai
Beth Swagman
Nicholas Vander Kwaak
Mary Vander Vennen
Mary Stewart Van Leeuwen
Thomas Zeyl

Abusive situations that are brought to light in the church situation are not the sole jurisdiction of the pastor and the council. All church members should consider the following suggestions regarding the problem of abuse.

Be Alert to Signals of Possible Sexual Abuse

1. An adult treating a particular child with extreme favoritism.

2. The "accidental" touching of a child's private parts or the rubbing of one's body against the child.

3. The suggestion that an adult should see and/or touch a child's body to monitor development.

4. The unnecessary application of lotion on a child's body.

5. The "accidental" intrusion of an adult into the bathroom or bedroom when a child is undressed, or failure to respect the child's right to privacy.

6. An adult's suggestion to a child that he or she is involved in sexual activities with other boys or girls.

7. An adult's attempt to teach a child about sex education by displaying pornography, showing off his or her body, or touching the child's body.

8. An adult's use of sexually suggestive language while referring to a child's body.

9. An adult's description of her or his sexual exploits to a child.

10. An adult's warning a child not to tell anyone about the things that happened or were discussed between the adult and the child.

11. An adult's "accidental" removal or opening of some or all of his or her clothing in the presence of a child.

Investigate; Don't Shy Away

It sometimes takes years of hesitation and mountains of courage for a survivor to tell her story. One of the most devastating results of finally sharing this pain with another is being met with disbelief or having her pain minimized because her account makes the listener uncomfortable. After such a reception, the victim may doubt the wisdom of sharing; she may regret her courage to tell and never do so again. No matter how ugly or seemingly improbable the story, do listen. Try to see past the details of the victim's pain. Even if the evidence seems to you to be contradictory, do not judge. It is vitally important that you not close a door that may have taken an abuse victim years to open.

Don't Overreact

Listen quietly and calmly; don't overreact. This may be the first time you have ever directly heard such a pain-filled story. If so, your reaction may be stronger than you realize. Monitor yourself as you listen. Don't let the focus of the account switch to you and your reaction; such a switch does not help the survivor.

Resist Judgment

It may be easy to condemn the abuser, but remember that your task is not to judge or pronounce sentence on the accused; that task is for others. Neither is it your task to dig up all the facts. You are not a court of law; you are a listener. Avoid drawing conclusions related to the problem. Avoid asking questions that are *not* directly related to the situation. Do not ask questions just for the sake of learning more details to satisfy your own curiosity. Deal only with the facts as stated, and keep the focus on how you can help. Questions like "Did you *deserve* it? or "Did you *let* him do this to you?" are inappropriately judgmental. Questions such as "How can I help?" or "What would you like me to do?" are supportive.

Ask About the Safety of Others

Are there minors who may still be at risk of the same abuse, such as schoolchildren, church school participants, or children in sports events? Is there a spouse at risk? Are any coworkers at risk? Your task here is simply to recognize the risks so that others may be mobilized to help. Minors, people who are older, and people who have physical or mental disabilities may be in urgent need of attention.

Do Not Try to Be a Therapist

"Unless you can help put people together again, don't take them apart" is a basic rule in counseling. Helping people come to terms with the past or the present is demanding and difficult work. This work is best left to qualified therapists. If you are asked to make a therapeutic diagnosis or to give a legal opinion, gently but firmly decline. Be empathetic to feelings and to the situation, but do not get into judgments about punishment or into an interpretation of the law. The information you provide may be confusing if, at a later date, these judgments or interpretations have to be changed.

Offer to Arrange for Professional Help

It is best for adult survivors to make their own arrangements for counseling. But, should they not be able to do so, do offer to help them get started. You may have to investigate and facilitate access to (preferably Christian) counselors, if such qualified individuals are available in your area.

Professional individual counseling should be started as soon as possible. The therapist will decide when spouses and/or children should be involved. Usually, transportation and finances will need to be discussed. You may need to help get diaconal support in arranging for these needs.

Ask What Else the Survivor Would Like You to Do

Before you go further, sit down and openly discuss what else the survivor would like you to do and the limits of what you can give. Sometimes a survivor wants only a listening ear. If the situation does not legally require notification of the authorities, you have more options. Which direction you should go will depend largely on the wishes of the victim.

Discuss Current and Past Church-related Help

Sometimes the church has been part of the problem. Therefore, going directly to the pastor or the council should not be an automatic response. Each situation must be clarified: Has the victim tried to discuss the problem with previous pastors and/or council members? What was their reaction? What does the survivor think of contacting the current pastor and/or council? Do not go against the needs of the survivor here. A good therapist will explore this area in-depth. If the church has been part of the problem, this difficulty must be dealt with before it can be part of the solution.

Notification

If the victim is a minor, you should notify the proper child-protection agency of your province or state, even if you are not legally required to do so. Usually, reporting knowledge of abuse is not merely an option; many provincial and state laws are quite specific that reporting is mandatory, so you should become fully acquainted with the relevant laws in your area. In most cases, failure to report can result in a penalty. Anonymity and confidentiality are assured. The problem of abuse cannot be solved solely within church boundaries.

Confrontation

Do not confront abusive parents if the victim is their minor child. The worker from the child-protection agency will take care of that. Unnecessary confrontation may result in angry exchanges that do not help anyone involved.

Lodging

If the victim is a minor, the child-protection agency must arrange for temporary lodging if it is needed. However, if you have already thought of lodging and can make arrangements, an agency will usually accept such an offer. It's useful to have such a strategy in place at the time you report to the agency.

Medical Intervention

If the abused person is a minor, the child-protection agency will seek medical attention or investigation. If the person is an adult and evidence of abuse needs to be documented, you may have to escort the victim to a doctor or to a local emergency room.

Confidentiality

Confidentiality is a must, whether the survivor is an adult or a minor. *The knowledge you have must be kept to yourself and not shared with anyone without the victim's consent,* unless the survivor is a child, and then it may be shared only with the child-protection agency. If council members need to consult with one another, they must remember not to identify a person. Unless assured that imminent danger is at hand or that a minor is involved, council members should refer anonymously to the people involved.

However, confidentiality should not be confused with secrecy. Secrecy implies concealment of the crime, which can be very damaging to a survivor. If you learn about an abuse case and do nothing with the information, you are inadvertently conspiring with the abuser, whose greatest wish is that no one find out.

Communication with Minors

Talk to a child in private if it is possible; under such circumstances, children may express themselves more freely. They may express themselves in ways that are unfamiliar to you. If you don't understand their messages, get help. It is important to remember that a child may have been previously threatened with severe consequences for "telling." Even many years after the abuse, such threats may act as a barrier to telling anyone about the crime. A therapist may have to be the one to unravel the story; some therapists are better trained than others for doing so. Do consult with agencies or professionals in the area to find an experienced counselor.

Dealing with Abusers

Communication with alleged abusers is difficult. Adopt a nonjudgmental approach and be supportive. Abusers hurt too, even if they don't consciously admit to it. Do not discuss the alleged events with them; usually they attempt to minimize what happened. Avoid agreeing to quick resolutions; these are always too shallow and may cause the survivor additional pain. Do show empathy—others' reactions can be extremely important in facilitating an abuser's decision to seek counseling.

Church Policy Statements on Abuse

The following procedures were proposed to the Georgetown, Michigan, Christian Reformed Church (CRC) as the church's response to possible abuse situations. These are draft documents. We have included the church's general abuse policy and the specific procedures for church school. Georgetown CRC is also implementing procedures regarding its nursery and its preteen programs, Calvinettes and Cadets.

Georgetown Christian Reformed Church Abuse Policy

1. The staff, officers, leaders, teachers, or anyone in a position representing Georgetown Christian Reformed Church (hereafter referred to as Georgetown) are required to report any suspected or alleged incidences of abuse to the senior pastor or his designee. It is not the responsibility of the reporting person to substantiate the alleged abuse, but only to report it to the senior pastor. When the alleged victim is a minor, the reporting person will be encouraged to report this to the local children's protective services agency.

    The church council requires the senior pastor to report all alleged abuse cases involving minor children to children's protective services. It is our church's responsibility to cooperate fully with children's protective services and with law-enforcement agencies.

    Maintaining records of reported incidences will be left to the discretion of the pastor staff, but if such records are kept they must be secure and confidential.

2. All staff, leaders and teachers at Georgetown will be mandated to attend an educational seminar on the dynamics of all types of abuse; this will include the church's policies and how to recognize signs of abuse and inappropriate behavior.

3. Each program in Georgetown that involves children is required to have and maintain operating procedures that will prevent and protect children from being abused.

4. In order to assure protection for children and to prevent abuse from happening, all adult positions at Georgetown (both paid and volunteer) will be screened for previous abuse offenses. This screening will include a volunteer profile form, references, a criminal record clearance, and an interview by the pastor staff.

5. All children and youth will be informed of these policies through their programs. All children will receive information on how to protect themselves and who they can consult for help. Parents will be invited to these classes and attendance records will be maintained.

6. Hall monitors will be available during church services and Sunday school hour. Two trained and dedicated people should be assigned for each service for a one-month period. The morning-service monitors would also serve during the Sunday school hour.

7. An abuse team should be formed that would be trained in ministering to victims and offenders. We recommend that this team be composed of the senior pastor, an administrative elder, a pastoral elder, and up to three knowledgeable and aware members of the congregation.

8. Removal or suspension of alleged offenders serving in some capacity within the church will follow the listed guidelines:

    a. When the allegation is made of abuse, the alleged offender must be confronted with the allegations by either the senior pastor or by a designated appointee from the pastoral elders, and must be suspended from participating in all service roles in the church.

    b. If the allegations are found to be false, the censure on service will be lifted.

    c. If the allegations are found to be true, the offender must continue under censure and be dealt with by the pastoral elders per Church Order articles 78 through 94.

9. Reinstatement of a healed offender will follow the listed guidelines:

    a. The ex-offender must request reinstatement into the church and admit sorrow for this sin per Church Order articles 84, 87, 93, and 94.

b. The healed offender must submit a psychologist's or therapist's statement of visitation and progress in treatment on a regular basis to the senior pastor or to his designee.

c. A healed offender will not be placed in a volunteer position that places him at risk.

Sunday School Procedures
Children's Worship and Little People's church

1. All teachers must fill out the volunteer profile and be interviewed by the pastor staff.

2. All teachers are required to attend the abuse-education class.

3. The first week of Sunday school will be a training week. Students and teachers will receive an explanation of all rules (geared to all age groups). This will be done with both students and teachers present, so both groups are aware of each other's rules.

4. Any one-on-one outings (student with teacher) will require written notification to the Sunday school superintendent or the youth pastor, and must include the student's name, the date, the time, and the purpose of the trip. There must also be a follow-up call to the student and teacher for a progress report (see footnote).

5. Hall monitors must check the hallways and bathrooms during Sunday school.

6. Anyone not following the rules stated must be reported to the superintendent and the pastor staff.

Bathroom Procedure for Children's Worship and Little People's Church

1. Always use the same bathroom.

2. No boys may take children to the bathroom.

3. The person attending the child must sign him or her out when they leave and back in when they return.

Note: Establishing a rule for always having two people with each child gets complicated. If enforced, such a rule can prohibit teachers from building trusting, one-on-one relationships with their students, especially with suspected victims. Allowing a teacher to take a child alone for a quiet chat could set the child up for abuse, but *not* allowing this one-on-one relationship may keep children from having a chance to learn trust and possibly share an already abusive experience.

We feel that the notification rule protects both teacher and child, and the follow-up calls show concern for both parties. Following up on these meetings is *very important*. No teacher may ever take a student alone without advance notification. Students must be asked if they want to have another visit with the teacher, and must be given permission to say no if they choose. Without proper follow-up procedures, a rule of two people with every child would be required.